MW00412188

Glossary

1.	Grand Babies And Old Farts	5
2.	School Dazes	11
3.	Plain Ole Dumb	17
4.	Mad Man	21
5.	Big Moe	27
6.	Fishing For Chickens	33
7.	Fixin To Go Racing	43
8.	Lord Of The Flies	61
9.	He Throws Like A Girl	67
10.	No Brakes, No Problem	71
11.	Daytona USA	75
12.	Knuckles	89
13.	No Bucks, No Buck Rogers	95
14.	Black Belt, Black Belt!	99
15.	Coon Heads	109
16.	Dad and Mom	119
17.	Another Bob	129
18.	My Bride	135
19.	Sand In My Shoes	139
20.	Billy	147
21.	The Banjo Man	153
22.	Chicken Crap	157

The Life and Times of a Good Ole Boy

Chapter 1

Grand Babies and Old Farts

I live in Wilkes County, North Carolina. It's where, strange enough, *Lowe's* got started. But, I'll go into that later. Its heritage is mostly known for moonshine and stock car racing. At one time it was known as the "Moonshine capital of the world." I'm sure there are folks in other places in the South that would argue that. No doubt, some would even fight over it. It's funny what people take pride in. I guess everybody takes pride in whatever they got.

Couple miles north of my place, we've got a restaurant called *Carol's*. They took an old, singlewide mobile home, knocked out a few walls and put up a sign. Don't look for franchises; the only expansion plan they keep talking about is knocking down that third bedroom wall. But then they wouldn't know what to do with all the junk.

I told 'em if they could ever get *American Pickers* to stop by, they could make more money off junk than hamburgers.

A few summers ago, I was in there eating lunch. A couple of "'Ole farts" came in to eat. ('Ole farts are men that are about twenty years older than you are, it doesn't matter how old you are.) Being from the South, you would never call an elderly lady an "'Ole fart," unless she did something really offensive - like having a politically correct bumper sticker on her car, but that ain't likely to happen around here.

I wasn't trying to overhear their conversation, but they were talking about terrorism. One of them said,

"If they blow themselves up, they get forty virgins."

The other one said, "I think it's seventy."

The first one said, "Well, hell. I guess we don't have to worry about 'em blowing up anything in Wilkes County."

"Probably not, but they are some mean SOBs."

"Yeah, but if it was twenty degrees hotter and I didn't have any toilet paper, I might want to blow something up myself."

Not only did they not laugh, they barely smiled. Well, I laughed enough for all three of us.

A few months later, I was in the Captain's chair watching TV. I call it the Captain's chair because I'm in charge. That's because my wife, Tracy, told me I could be.

My oldest daughter, Katy, and her boyfriend (now husband, Adam) rolled up, came in the house and said, "We need to talk to you and Momma."

Well, Ray Charles could see where this was going,

"I'm pregnant."

Tracy gave a sigh.

Overhearing the conversation, my youngest daughter Casey, came out of her bedroom and said, "Me too."

Tracy hung her head.

Having been given the gift of always knowing what to say, I said, "Well, I guess you know you just killed your mother."

Not getting the positive response I had hoped for, I patted my wife on the back and said, "Well, at least we're doing our part to fight terrorism in Wilkes County."

Looking back, that might not have been the right thing either, so before I did any more damage, I turned off the TV and went to bed. The next day I met my three brothers at *Cracker Barrel*. When my oldest brother John got there, I was already eating.

"I guess you heard I'm going to be a grandpa?"

He too, having the gift, let these magic words roll off his tongue,

"Well, ninety percent of the adult population is having sex, and the other ten percent wish they were."

I don't know if it was the words of wisdom or the coffee, but I felt better. When I got home I thought I would try again. I told Tracy what John had said. She hesitated while it soaked in a couple seconds, then she said, "What's that supposed to mean?"

Now it was my turn to reflect a couple seconds.

"I don't know, it sounded better when I heard it than when I said it."

She just looked at me.

Then I said, "Would you like me to make a pot of coffee?"

I knew I had said the right thing when she said, "Yeah, that sounds good."

I guess the point I am trying to make is we're all going through life with difficult situations, and we're just trying to make the best of them. What was a difficult thing at the time are now the cutest grandkids in the world saying, "We want Pawpaw!"

Like I said, "Wilkes County is known for racing."

The first time I ever went to a stock car race was in 1960. We could hear the cars practicing from our house, so Dad took me and John to North Wilkesboro Speedway. I fell in love with it right off the bat. The local hero was Junior Johnson.

Let me stop right here and say something that needs to be said: I get aggravated every time I'm watching some kind of sporting event on TV and somebody asks somebody, "Who was your idol when you were young?"

An idol is something you worship, so my idol is Jesus Christ. My hero growing up, for the most part, was Richard Petty. Now, Richard is called, "The King," but if you were to ask him, he would tell you the same thing I'm getting ready to tell you. There's only one "King of Kings," and he ain't him.

And, while we're on the subject, let me go on and say

early in this book, I love Jesus and he loves me, and I don't make no apologies for it.

Now back to Junior. Junior's nickname was "The Wilkes County Wild Man," but for some reason I liked "Fireball Roberts." I don't remember why. I guess when you're six, how could you not like a guy that's named "Fireball"?

I knew from then on I wanted to be a racecar driver. When I was nine, my dad took me over to Charlotte Motor Speedway to the *World 600*. Early in the race there was a big crash. Strange how after almost fifty years I can still see it like it happened yesterday. I can still see that huge ball of fire in my mind. We didn't know what cars were involved, but when the wreckers started hauling the cars off my dad was looking through binoculars and said, "It's Fireball, I don't see how he could still be alive."

I remember looking through the binoculars with tears in my eyes. I don't know if that was the right thing to say to a nine year old, but it was the truth. People seemed to be tougher back then. A few days later he lost his life due to third degree burns.. From then on, I started liking Richard.

10

Chapter 2

School Dazes

Now, when I decided to write this book, I decided to tell it like it is, or was to the best of my recollection. The good, the bad or whatever, and let the chips fall where they may.

I've noticed over the years, people tend to enjoy the things they're good at. Pardon my language, but having said this, I damn near hated school with a passion. Speaking just for me, I found it to be aggravating, boring, and way too time consuming. And that was its good attributes.

Fortunately, most people don't share my experience. I was a few years younger than my brother John, who just happened to be one of those, straight "A" students. More than once on the first day of school, a teacher would see my last name and ask, "Are you Johnny Stowe's brother?"

I would say, "Yes."

And they would act all excited.

Within a few days they would say something like, "We must be talking about a different Johnny Stowe. You can't be his brother."

When I got to the seventh grade, I was called to the guidance counselor's office. I didn't even know there was such a thing. He wanted me to put some puzzles together while he held a stopwatch.

When I finished he asked me if I had ever seen these puzzles before. When I told him no, he said that was as fast as anybody had ever put them together. So, then he showed me a picture of a triangle interlocked into a circle and told me to draw it. When I finished, he seemed pretty impressed. I couldn't understand why; it seemed pretty simple. It was kinda' fun, but I really didn't know the purpose of all this so he sent me back to class.

A couple of weeks later, they said they wanted to send me to something called the "Learning Academy." Supposedly, it was designed for boys who should be performing better in school, but for some reason weren't.

When I got there, I realized I had made a mistake. If I could have taken the test over, I would have performed more like Forest Gump. What they called the "Learning Academy" should have been called a "Juvenile Delinquent Reform School for Misfits."

I couldn't really see the purpose or the strategy of the place. About halfway through my tour of duty, one of the teachers said he was going to divide the class into two groups. He said this group is starting to make progress academically and this other group, of which I was included, was still under achieving and having a problem with discipline and causing problems in class. As he said this, he glanced over at me and said, "I am going to divide this group again. You really don't cause any trouble; you just sit there like some fruit or vegetable."

So you're all by yourself. Looking back, I was a misfit for being at the school in the first place, and then I was a misfit among misfits. And then, I didn't even fit into that group. In the whole county I had managed to be singled out. I guess some people would have been scarred for life, but for me it was just another day at school.

When I was in the 9th grade, the teacher gave us a pop test. It was just a true-false test. I figured based on the laws of mathematical probability I should get at least half of them right.

Unfortunately, it wasn't a math class. It was English. Now, this is the only test I ever took in school where I noticed the guy beside me was trying to copy my answers. At lunch I asked him why he was trying to copy my paper.

He said he wasn't. He said he didn't know which answers were right, but he felt pretty sure I would be wrong, so he just answered opposite of me. I made a D, and he made a B. But, the truth is he just got lucky. He didn't know it, but I didn't read the questions. I just circled the answers.

That same year, math proved to be just as difficult. Now about half way through the year, me and my math teacher finally reached a mutual agreement. I wouldn't bother her, if she would do the same for me.

My English teacher would give me her newspaper every day, and my math teacher would let me set at the back of the class and read it as long as I didn't make too much noise turning the pages. Now, this was last period and one day she said unless everybody quieted down they would have to stay after class.

I guess they didn't take her seriously because when the bell rang everybody got up to leave. She said, "All right, everybody sit back down. You're staying 10 extra minutes."

"Except for Joel; we don't consider you part of the class. You can go."

I can still see Frank Tingly's wide-open mouth as I walked out the door. She was one of the few teachers I got along with.

In the 12th grade, they decided to sell bottles of soap to raise money for uniforms for the football team. It might have been uniforms for the band. It was a long time ago, and I really don't remember. One thing I'm sure of. I didn't care anymore then than I do now. The teachers gave everybody one bottle to use as a sales sample. At PE class everyday they would call your name at roll call, and if you sold any soap, you would say the number you had sold.

If you hadn't sold any, you would just say, "Here."

This went on for a few weeks and every day I would say the same thing, "Here."

Well, as it turned out, my sister Jane said she would

wash my car one Saturday. She said she needed some soap. I told her there was a bottle in the floorboard of the back seat.

On Monday morning, when the roll was called at PE, the gym teacher was going through the usual routine, when he said, "Stowe," I said, "One."

There was an instant roar from my fellow classmates, followed by a standing ovation. The teacher didn't want to waste the opportunity to give a motivational speech.

He said, "If Stowe can sell one bottle, the rest of us should be able to sell at least 100 bottles."

Once again a roar came from the crowd. I figured by only selling one bottle, I might have sold a thousand.

It's like they say, "The Lord works in mysterious ways."

In the 12th grade I was called to the office one day. There wasn't anything unusual about that. But what was unusual was that I had no idea why.

The principal sat me down in his office and said he was going through all the seniors' records and said, "You're four credits short of being able to graduate."

I thought there must be some mistake; it has to be more than that. How many do you have to have, five?

"Well, regardless of how many," he said, "We don't want you around here next year any more than you want to be here." This was the first time in 12 years we were in total agreement. No, actually it was 13.

If I'm going to have to do the time, I'm going to get credit for it.

He said, "If you go to summer school and pass a class in English, I'll pass you under one condition." My ears were wide open. "Don't say anything about it. I could get in trouble."

I said, "Say anything about what?"

Now, I know you're thinking. I just broke a promise. Technically, that's true. But, that was thirty-eight years ago and surely the statute of limitations has run out by now. Besides I don't think he is going to get in any real trouble since I saw in the paper he died about twenty years ago.

Chapter 3

Plain 'Ole Dumb

When I was in high school I started driving a school bus. This was 1973. Back then high school students could drive the bus in North Carolina. It was a pretty good deal. You got out of last period and got paid for it. You can't beat a deal like that.

Anyway, that's where I met a bus mechanic named Bob Powell. Him and another guy, Joe Simmons, had a dirt track racecar. I knew this was my chance to get into racing.

Before I go on about my racing career, let me tell you about some things that happened when I was driving a school bus. I was dropping some elementary kids off from school. Now the way we are supposed to do it is, stop the bus, let the kids get up, and then they leave the bus. I decided early on that this was too slow. So, I had the next bunch that was to get off to stand in the aisle. As soon as we stopped and the door opened, they could get off.

I opened the door and some kids got off. I shut the door and started down the road. I could hear screaming, but it was kind of faint. I looked in the mirror above my head at the kids, but couldn't locate the screams.

Whatever, I just kept driving.

At top speed one of the girls in the aisle that was

blocking my view of the door yelled, "Look!"

Apparently a boy got off the bus and just stood there, or, I just shut the door to soon. But whatever the case, I trapped the back of his coat in the door. He was on the outside of the bus with his arms and legs flapping. I hit the brakes, slowed down to three or four miles per hour and opened the door. He hit the ground and rolled over in a yard. Although he was probably only in the third grade, he got up ready to fight and yelled something at me. I couldn't understand what he said, but it didn't really matter. I figured the damage was done, so I just kept going. I heard a rock hit the back of the bus.

I figured that was the end of my bus driving career, but I never heard anything. I always wondered what became of that kid. Now that whole thing from my point of view was just bad luck for me and the kid. Let's face it; it could have happened to anybody, but looking back, this next story had nothing to do with luck.

I've tried to figure out a way to blame it on something else, but it just keeps coming out just "plain-'ole-dumb."

I tried to figure out a way to lift it up to the next level: "ignorant." But it just keeps rolling back down the hill to just "plain-'ole-dumb."

When this book comes out and it hits the big time and at least a hundred copies are in print, I don't know what people are going to say. I'm sure some may never talk to me again. That's one of the reasons I wrote it. But, nobody will say he can dish it out, but he can't take it.

Okay, try this. After a couple days of heavy rain, the creeks had become rivers. After me and the other young terrorists, also known as "school bus drivers," had dropped off our fellow kids. We rode around looking at all the flood damage. We rode down to Gum Branch Road, where the top rail of the bridge was almost under water. Then this brilliant idea came to me. Probably right out of hell. *I think I will go back and get my bus and drive across.*

When I got back, the other terrorists were up on the hill anxiously awaiting my return. Now, I've heard extensive studies have been done on different personality types about their last thoughts.

For idiots, it's almost always "Watch this!"

I knew if I was going to be able to make it all the way across I was going to have to carry some real speed. I hit it wide open! A wall of water surged halfway up the windshield. I was at least smart enough to know the wipers were useless.

I know it's hard to believe, but I didn't make it. School buses run on gas and air, not gas and water. She conked out in the middle of the bridge. Water started pouring in through the door.

I blame that on that kid's coat; it messed up the seal. To keep from getting wet I had to raise my feet to the top of the pedals. I thought I might just abandon ship and just swim for it, but I soon realized I might drown. The world probably would have been a better place - especially for taxpayers. I didn't want to panic. I decided to reason it all out. I should have done that a half hour ago. I thought, it's Friday, and I'll just sit tight till Monday morning if necessary. By then surely the water will have receded, and I can just drive out of here. Then, an even more brilliant idea came to me. I was on a roll. *Just put it in first gear and ride the starter.* It worked!

She slowly moved forward. Not knowing which would come first, the end of the water, or the end of the battery. Here's where luck came back into it.

I made it! After the engine conked for fifteen minutes or so, she came back to life. I told my fellow terrorist later that if I had to do it all over again, I wouldn't have done it. Because, that bus never ran the same again. It lost two or three miles per hour for the rest of the year.

For some reason they don't let kids drive the buses anymore. It seemed like a good program to me. Now back to my racing career.

Chapter 4

Mad Man

I knew before I could drive a racecar I'd have to pay my dues. So, I decided to help Bob and Joe at a track in Monroe, North Carolina. The name of it was Starlite Speedway. Now it's a housing development.

I've been around racing for fifty years. But, on August 3, 1973, I saw the worst wreck I'd ever seen. A driver from Rockingham North Carolina named James Sears got tapped by another car and lost control.

There was a split in the guardrail to allow vehicles into the infield. His car went into it and hit the end of the guardrail. His car was cut in half and exploded. What was left rolled down the track and was run over by some other cars. Everybody on pit road ran to the wreck. He was under another car that's gas tank had exploded. There was a frantic attempt to put out the fire, but everyone knew it was futile. It's the first time I ever saw someone die.

I'll never forget the smell and seeing them put Sears in a body bag and drive off.

No sirens, no lights. Realizing ten minutes earlier he was full of life. Doing what he loved, and now he's gone.

I grew up a lot that night. I don't know why, but for

some reason I still wanted to drive. Over the winter, I found an old fifty-six Chevy that was converted into a racecar.

My first race was in Gaffney South Carolina. My mom and dad didn't want to go that far to see me race. But my mom asked me before I left if I had on clean underwear.

"Mom, why do I need clean underwear?"

"Because if you get in a wreck and have to go to the hospital, I want you to have on clean underwear."

So, with her blessing and clean underwear, I was off!

I stopped by and got Bob. Now Bob was in the Army in World War II. To prove it, he had scars where a German machine gun put five bullets through him. He was as crazy as he was tough.

If you ever saw the movie *Paint Your Wagon*, he was just like Ben Rumson, played by Lee Marvin. Before we go on with the trip, let me tell you some of the stuff Bob did.

He had a shop in his backyard with a fence around it. He had an old mule, and I asked him why he kept a mule. He said he likes to sneak up on it and kick it in the ass.

"Sometimes I kick him, and sometimes he kicks me."

Now when somebody tells you something either you believe it or you don't. There are basically two things to consider: Who said it, and what they said. Like, if a politician says it you automatically assume they're lying. If they're liberal democrat, you know they're lying.

Now, with this said I figure Bob would probably try to sneak up on a mule. I just didn't know if it's possible. A mule is bound to have good hearing with those big ears. Another time, he sold a guy an old engine that he knew was outside around the shop somewhere, but they couldn't find it. He said they kicked leaves for fifteen minutes before they found it. Again, it could have gone either way. I figured the truth was probably somewhere in the middle. I figured five to ten minutes!

Bob had some Yankees that moved in beside him, I felt sorry for 'em. Let me clarify. I felt sorry for all of 'em, especially the Yankees.

One night Bob's mule got out and was in their yard. The head Yankee came out screaming at Bob.

As I expected, this wasn't going to end very well. Bob went over and didn't say a thing. The next morning it was tied to their mailbox and Bob was sitting on his porch with a shotgun.

When the head Yankee came out screaming, Bob blew his mailbox off the post. It was all settled out of court when Bob agreed to pay for the damages. So, it all ended better than I thought it would. I noticed later on there was a different bunch of cars in front of that house. I asked Bob what the deal was. "They moved out last week; he must have gotten transferred or something." I kind of leaned toward the "or something."

Bob's kid came home one time with some homework. His teacher wanted him to draw a picture of a dinosaur tooth and identify the different parts. How many parts could there be to a dinosaur tooth? This agitated Bob to no end.

He said, "What the ---- are they teaching over there?" Why don't they teach them something they need to know, like the firing order of a small block Chevy?"

In case you might want to use this book to fix a car, it's 1-8-4-3-6-5-7-2.

He's undoubtedly the craziest man I've ever known. And you can ask my brothers; that's saying something.

Back now to our trip.

I don't remember much about the race, but the ride home was quite an adventure. By the time we got halfway home, Bob was wasted. He always drank *Papst Blue Ribbon Beer*. He looked up ahead and saw a Waffle House.

"Pull in here. I want some coffee and a burger."

I knew this wasn't going to go very well, but whatever happened, at least I had on "clean underwear"!

We went inside and sat down. The waitress walked by and then walked by again. Suddenly, Bob yelled out, "Hey lady, can we get waited on?"

She looked at him and said, "We're changing shifts right now sir."

He said, "Well, change shifts on your own ---- time!"

Well, they got into a screaming match. I don't know who was winning, but I know who was losing. Me!

Finally, he said, "Well, we'll take our business elsewhere."

I know they hated to see us leave about as much as I hated to go.

I remember thinking: *I'm glad that's over.*

After driving a few more miles he said, "I'm still hungry; pull in here."

It was Shoney's. I was just a kid and easily intimidated, especially by a madman. So we pulled in. We walked to the door, and he started pushing as hard as he could. The door said, "Pull."

But he started banging on the door and yelling, "Them SOBs down the road called up and told we were coming!"

The people inside looked as worried as I was. In desperation, I told him if he would go back to the truck, I would find a way in. To my surprise, he staggered back to the truck. I told the guy inside to get me a cup of coffee and a burger out here fast. I've never seen a Shoney's with such fast service.

When I got back to the truck, Bob complained about the food.

As we started to roll off, he started yelling, "Whoa!

Whoa!"

My first thought was the trailer had come loose. But when I looked in the mirror it was still there.

I said, "What's wrong?"

"Pull over to the curb. I want to throw some rocks at this place before we leave!" (Some people think Ernest T. Bass is far-fetched.)

That was it. I finally got the gonads to keep changing gears. All the way home he blamed me for everything.

He said, "Don't you ever take me to one of those high society places again!"

We pulled in his driveway about 3 AM. He got out and staggered towards the house. I remembered backing out of his driveway thinking that it was a lot of fun.

I went home and crawled into bed. About 8 o'clock my mom came in my room and said, "Bob's wife is on the phone."

Well, I didn't expect that.

I said, "Hello."

She asked, "Where is Bob?"

"I let him out about 3."

"Okay," she said and hung up.

A couple minutes later she called back and said she found him in the storage room on top of the chest freezer.

Chapter 5

Big Moe

Now at the time I was a truck driver delivering lumber for *Lowe's*. The warehouse manager was a guy named Big Moe Ham. Moe was a modern day mountain man from West Jefferson, North Carolina. He stood about 6'4" and 270 pounds. He was rather fond of moonshine and cigars.

He asked me one time if I wanted to go up to his place and go deer hunting. It wasn't what I expected. I thought I would be in a deer stand. Instead he, John, and I rode around most of the day in his blue '55 Chevy, with our guns hanging out the windows.

Somewhere along the journey I said, "I know this ain't legal. Aren't you worried about the game warden?"

Well, first off, it was a dumb question. Big Moe ain't never been worried about nothing!

But he said, "The game warden don't come up here no more. He got tired of getting shot at."

That made sense to me. I could understand the game warden's point of view, so we just kept hunting. Although it wasn't what I expected, we had a good time. And for the rest of the day we didn't see any deer, or game warden.

Before we get back to the subject of racing, I need to tell

you about a couple of other things that happened at work. Big Moe hired a new driver. The first day on the job they sent him to deliver a framing order to a golf course. The directions said to go to the second road on the right past the clubhouse. Well, unfortunately, the golf cart path crossed the road. He turned onto it. It had just rained and the truck was wider than the path. He was on the second fairway before the greens keeper could stop him.

I remember Big Moe wasn't happy that day. When the driver got back to the store, well, I'll just put it this way. I'm just glad I knew the difference between the two.

They sent me on a delivery up to Harrisburg. After I dropped the lumber, I went by Charlotte Motor Speedway. The gate was open. I couldn't resist the temptation. So, I drove in and started turning laps. The more laps I turned, the faster I got. Finally, I was wide open.

On about lap five some guy came running across the tri-oval waving his arms to stop me. He yelled, "What the hell do you think you're doing?"

I said, "I guess I'm lost."

What he said next, I can't repeat. When I got back to the store, Big Moe said, "Somebody called here saying one of our drivers was driving around the track, I didn't have to ask which one. I'd rather you not do that anymore."

Then there was one more. I saved the best for last. Big

Moe hired a guy that had just come back from Vietnam. He said he wanted to haul drywall. Nobody liked to haul drywall. So, Moe told him he could have all of it.

After a few weeks he was driving on I-85 crossing the Catawba River when he had a heart attack. The fellow that was riding with him grabbed the steering wheel and pulled over to the side of the interstate. He got out of the truck, walked about a half mile to the next exit and called back to the store. Big Moe wasn't there, so he told the assistant warehouse manager what happened. The warehouse manager then told him to walk back to the truck and he would meet him out there.

By the time they got to the truck, that poor 'ole boy was dead. So, these two geniuses put him in the trunk of the car and took him to the hospital. They drove up to the emergency room, went inside, and told the lady at the desk, "We've got a dead man in the trunk of the car."

To their surprise, she called the cops. After a few hours of questioning, the cops let them go back to work. I always wondered what people riding by thought when they saw two guys putting a dead man in a trunk.

Well, back to racing. Big Moe told me one day he wanted to start helping me at the track. Me and Bob were on pit road when we saw that blue '55 Chevy coming. He spun around and pulled in beside me.

I said, "They won't let you park here; you've got to park

in the infield."

It was obvious he had already gotten into his moonshine. He said, " I might run her a few laps."

When the deputy showed up he convinced him that wasn't going to happen and showed him where to park.

Mark Twain said, "Don't let the truth get in the way of a good story."

Well this ain't no story. This is the truth.

After we ran the heat race, Moe asked me who was driving that car over there. He pointed at Dale Earnhardt's car. Dale was still running dirt at the time.

I said, "Dale Earnhardt."

Big Moe said he didn't like his driving style. He didn't know it at the time, but millions of others would say the same thing in years to come. Moe walked over to him. I couldn't hear what he said, but I could see him throwing liquor in his face. Now Dale was the, "Intimidator", but he wasn't stupid. He didn't want to tangle with Big Moe unless he had to. After a brief confrontation with Dale's crew, here came the Sheriff's Department.

This time there were two deputies. They escorted Big Moe out of the track. After that night I knew if I was going to keep racing I was going to have to rethink this thing. If we were going to a bar room brawl I had the right bunch. But if I was going to keep racing, I would need a new crew. Of course back then sometimes you would go to a fight and a race would break out. Most of these little fellows today wouldn't have survived back then. But the whole thing kind of worked itself out.

I didn't see Big Moe again until Monday morning. He said he'd been barred from the track, and if he tried to come back he would be arrested. He said that was fine by him. The whole thing had left a bad taste in his mouth. I figured that taste was still at least 80 proof. Shortly after that Bob lost interest. I'm pretty sure with their age and lifestyles, they are gone ,but certainly not forgotten.

Chapter 6
Fishing For Chickens

In 1977, I went to a Winston Cup race. It was called Grand National back then. In the racing program I noticed a guy named Baxter Price. He was from Monroe, North Carolina. Not too far from me.

After the race I went down to pit road and started talking to him. I asked if he needed any free help at night. He said he could always use some free help.

Let me stop here for a minute and point out something. Today, me and my brothers build engine-testing facilities, primarily for race teams. I'm amazed at how many people these teams have. No wonder it cost so much to race anymore. Just the payroll alone is in the millions. We ran the full cup schedule with two or three full- time people.

But anyways, that's where I met my best friend Billy. You'll hear a lot more about Billy. We were young, traveling all over the country, mostly in the South. That was the country as far as we were concerned. We were going to different races every week and having the time of our lives.

All the pit crews were volunteers, and they would show up the night before the race. We would have five or six people in the hotel room. We were at the Richmond race and the guy I was sharing a bed with rolled over in the middle of the night, put his arm over me, and said, "Honey."

I said, "What?"

That 'ole boy came straight up in the bed! All he knew at that point was that: That *what*, didn't roll off the lips of his bride. He looked around with that *what in hell is going on look*, got his bearings, and dozed back off.

Along about the same time, a friend, Bobby Penniger was getting out of the Navy. We had become friends in high school when we were both driving school buses. He was deployed on the carrier J.F.K. as a metal fabricator.

He said it was mostly uneventful. Except for one day when he was told to make a weld at the base of a wall. He was required to have a spotter on the other side. So, he knocked on the door. He was told he had to have special clearance to enter that room.

He thought to himself: *It's a small weld. Nobody will know the difference.*

About the time he finished welding he heard someone on the other side yell, "Fire!" Then every alarm on the ship went off.

The ship's PA system started blaring; *General Quarters*, and five thousand men started scrambling. Except for one, who just dropped his head because he knew his ass was grass. He went up on a Court Marshall charge. He said he had visions of Leavenworth, but because of his good record they gave him a good tongue-lashing and some extra duty.

Well anyway, with his metal fabrication experience and my background in racing, we decided to make a go at building racecars, *without any government assistance*, I might add.

I knew a guy named Kenny Thompson. He's the best fabricator I've ever known. He worked for Ron Osterlund Racing. That's the team Dale Earnhardt got his first big time ride with. With his connections we got a big break right off the bat and started building their racecar chassis. The first time I talked to Dale in their shop he didn't bring up the subject of Big Moe, and I sure wasn't going to bring it up!

Anyway, Osterland Racing had a small building in their racing complex that was empty. So, we worked out a deal to rent it from them. We came up with the name *Dixie Engineering*. We thought it had a nice ring to it.

The general manager of the place was a guy named Roland. We started in the winter of 1979. As most small businesses it started out kinda' slow, but we managed to make payroll. When warmer weather came around we discovered the air conditioner wasn't working. After several complaints to Roland to fix it, it became apparent he had more important things to do than to mess with us. So on Saturday, when nobody else was around, Bobby decided to bring his ladder from home and fix it himself. I was in the shop building a chassis while he was on the roof. At lunch I asked him how it was going.

He said, "I just about have it fixed." Then he added, "If the racecar deal doesn't work out, it's always good to know you've got something else to fall back on."

When lunch was over, Bobby went back on the roof while I went back to welding. A couple minutes later he ran back in the building yelling, "Fire extinguisher, fire extinguisher!"

After the smoke and the fire extinguisher all blew away, I told him I thought he was referring to air conditioning repair to fall back on, not firefighting. He decided to put the cover back on and deny everything. In just two years, he had managed to almost burn down our building and sink an aircraft carrier.

We didn't stay there but a few more months. We felt the rent was too high, especially for a place that didn't have air conditioning. Anyway, we found an old building in Waxhaw, North Carolina to work out of.

There was an old country store up the road where we bought our gas and stuff. The guy that ran it was quite a character, even by my standards. Tragically, they found him hung behind it one morning with his hands duct taped behind his back.

On the news that night, the Sheriff said, "At this point, we're not ruling out foul play."

That eased the mind of everyone in the community,

knowing that with him handling the case it would be a matter of days before somebody was apprehended. That was thirty-one years ago. At this point, I think the only thing I am still hoping for is a deathbed confession.

The guy we rented the shop from was a fellow named Ralph. It was a run-down building beside his house, and it was only 3,000 square feet. He only let us use about two-thirds of it because he needed somewhere to put his junk. We put up a dividing wall and got started.

Every day at 3:05 in the afternoon we would take a break and watch the old black and white *Andy Griffith* show. We called it "3:0 Fife." Some people think America started a downhill trend when J.F.K. died. They're wrong. It's when *Andy Griffith* went from black and white to color. We went from Barney, Gomer, and Ernest T. Bass, to Warren, Emmett, and Howard Sprague. That's not downhill; that's falling off a cliff!

After a few months somebody tried to break in, but got scared off before they could get anything. So being single, I just set up a small place in the back and moved in. We called it "The Hole."

Everything was rolling along pretty smoothly until the day Ralph decided to get a rooster and a few chickens. Every morning at 3:45 AM, that damn rooster would crow! Until then, I thought roosters only crowed at the crack of dawn. I guess he was either real dumb or just warming up. He was only about three feet from my head on the other side of the dividing wall, and just about the time I dozed off, he would let'er rip again.

This went on for about three nights, until one morning, I said, "That's it!
There's going to be an ass kicking right now!"

The only way I could get to him was to walk all the way around the shop, so I put on my cowboy boots and started walking. There weren't any lights on that side of the building, but I could see the rooster's silhouette. Let me put it this way: I could barely see him. I needed something to attack him with. The only thing that was close that I could find in the dark was a fishing rod.

I swung at him and knocked the crap out of him! He took off out the door. About that time, the fishing line came off the reel. I started reeling him in. Have you ever found yourself in one of those situations where you think, "How did I get here?" Well, I was there! It was four o'clock in the morning, in the dead of winter, and I was standing outside in the dark in my underwear with cowboy boots on, holding a fishing rod, fishing for chickens. And, I caught one!

When I got him up to me I wasn't going to make a bad situation worse by getting spurred by no rooster. I was too smart for that. So, I cut the line and went back to bed. When it got light, I looked out the window. He had a hook in his neck and was all tangled up in the line trying to stand up.

When Ralph came around, I told him it looked like his rooster had gotten into his stuff, and he probably needed to get rid of him. I don't think he bought it.

There wasn't a whole lot of stuff going on in Waxhaw. It was known for antique furniture. We used to say the economy had gotten so bad that they had to shut down the antique factory and were just trying to sell off what they had left.

There were only two restaurants in town. One of the names I can't remember, and the other I wish I could forget. A single man needs a good place to eat. Now, just like they shut down the kids driving school busses, they shut down the good restaurant. And the one I was trying to forget stayed open. Without any options, me and one of my younger brothers, Jody, ventured in. The waitress handed us menus. I don't mind when food sticks to my ribs, but I'd prefer the menus didn't stick to my fingers.

She asked us what we would like to drink.

Jody said, "Tea."

She wrote it down.

I said, "Water."

She said, "The water has mud in it because the utility department has been working on the water lines."

Jody said, "Then how did you make the tea?"

Searching for the answer that never came, she just giggled. Then she said, "We've got soda in a can."

"I believe that's what we want." I said.

When the food came out it was about what I expected. It was neither good, nor bad. Just food.

When we had just gotten started good, she hollered to the cook through one of those openings between the kitchen and the rest of the world. "The ice machine is hung up again!"

A guy moseyed out of the kitchen. If you're not from the South, to mosey means to go somewhere in absolutely no hurry what so ever. The best I've seen is a good 'ole boy that's an engine builder at Richard Childress's named Sy. He has perfected it to an art form. Even the name fits. Matter of fact; if you looked up mosey in the dictionary his picture might be beside it.

His apron looked like it hadn't been washed since the grand opening, and I know they had been there at least two years. He walks into the men's room. I was impressed. If you're going to work on an ice machine, you need clean hands. He came out with a toilet plunger, walked to the machine, opened the lid, and started wailing!

When Bob had said, "Don't ever take me to one of those high society places again." I thought, what could be less high society than a waffle house. We just found it!

They had a Grade "A" sign on the wall. I wonder how many people have to die before you fail. I never would have thought I would say this, but I wish Bob woulda been there.

Needless to say, we left hungry.

Chapter 7

Fixin' To Go Racing

By this time I had been helping Baxter on a volunteer basis for about two years. I decided one day to ask him if I could drive just one race. I knew it was a long shot, but I figured a "No" would be the same as not asking. It would be kind of like handing your neighbor's sixteen-year-old the keys to your Mercedes, knowing he was going to drive down the road at 150 miles per hour for four hours, and then telling him before he leaves to be careful.

But then again, as lousy of a golfer as I am the only way I'll ever make a hole-in-one is to swing at the ball. I had nothing to lose. I didn't even know if he would take me seriously. They say timing is everything, so when I felt it was right, I asked.

He answered, "You've helped me a lot over the past few years without being paid for it. Let me talk to Patsy."

Patsy was his wife. Not only did he not laugh, it was actually up for consideration. Let me explain a little from my point of view what lay in the balance. A movie was made in 1973 about the life of Junior Johnson. Jeff Bridges played Junior. At one point in the movie everybody was trying to discourage him in his dream of racing.

Finally, one day his dad told him, "What's foolish for one man, is breath of life to another."

His dad's encouragement gave him the drive to push on. I was in the shop working on the racecar while Baxter was in the house. Now, I kind of know how it feels to be on trial while waiting on the jury to make a decision. He came out with a verdict. They had reached a decision. And it was, "Do you want to drive Dover?"

To get the opportunity to drive a Winston Cup Car to a racecar driver is like a guy and his guitar walking onto the stage at the *Grand 'Ole Opry* for the first time, or a kid who has practiced golf all his life teeing his ball up for his first *PGA* tournament. Although I tried not to show emotion on the outside, I was smiling ear to ear on the inside.

I know you find it hard to believe, but I said, " Sounds good to me."

What I felt inside all week was something I haven't felt since I was ten on Christmas Eve. Now, I hadn't driven a racecar in about two years, and all that was on dirt. My first asphalt race was going to be a five hundred mile cup race.

Now, the way it usually works is you start on a local track. Win races then move up to the next division and hope you eventually get a cup ride. At that rate I don't know which would have come first, the nursing home or a cup ride. I figured they had their way of doing things, and I had mine. Damn the torpedoes, full speed ahead!

When it was time to pack, I got out my old driving uniform. Originally, it had red stripes. But, my mom had washed it so many times over the years the stripes had turned pink. So with the pink suit, and a few extra pairs of clean underwear, I was gone.

When I saw the track for the first time, I took a deep breath and said, "Piece a cake." I think my brain was trying to catch the butterflies that were in my belly. When the first practice session started, I figured I would wait and let most of the cars get off the track.

Now, with all the high-speed asphalt racing experience I had, which was a total of five laps at *Charlotte Motor Speedway* in a lumber truck, I ventured onto the track. If I could handle a lumber truck wide open around Charlotte, I should be able to handle this.

I used the same strategy; I started out easy and got faster. The more laps I turned, the faster I got. This time on lap five they didn't black flag me, bring me in, and ask me, "What the hell do you think you're doing?"

I looked in the mirror down the backstretch and saw Dale coming up behind me. When he went around me in turn four, there must have been at least an inch between our cars. His left rear bumper clicked my right front. I thought, "Is he crazy or is he that good?" Or, is this finally retaliation for Big

Moe? I think it was the first two.

I was surprised at how well the car handled. One thing I've learned over the years is that a good racecar can make an average driver look pretty good. And, a bad car can make a good driver look pretty bad. Well, I qualified thirty-third out of forty. Not great, but we were in the race. That's all I cared about.

The night before the race me and my youngest brother, Jeff, and Billy shared a room. Jeff was only about sixteen, so me and him stayed in the room and went to bed early. Billy went out to parts unknown.

I was in one bed and Jeff was in the other. As anxious as I was, I was still able to fall asleep pretty fast. A couple hours later, here comes Billy. Now, you think he would get in the bed with Jeff since he only weighed about a hundred and fifty pounds. But no, he decided to get in the bed with the guy that weighed two hundred and twenty pounds - me!

I didn't go to sleep the rest of the night. It was like trying to sleep with the Tasmanian devil: flipping and flopping, moaning and groaning. That was thirty-one years ago and occasionally I still remind him of it.

After a sleepless night of looking at the ceiling, we were fixin' to go racin'. For you Yankees, that means it's race day. Just in case of a bad wreck, I put on clean underwear and headed over to the track.

When I got to the track, I went into the truck and put on my fire suit. When I came out, Billy started laughing.

"What are you laughing at?" I asked.

"The way you got your fire suit stuffed down inside your cowboy boots!"

"Billy, that's the way Richard's got his."

He said, "That's Richard. That ain't you. You look like Briscoe Darling in long johns. Pink stripes, cowboy boots and STP sticker."

I guess as long as Billy's around, I will always be paying my dues.

When they called my name at driver introductions, I stepped up on stage. The roar was deafening. I thought for a second I could hear somebody clapping. I figured it was John and his wife, Donna, who were up in the stands. But, that couldn't be right. They would be pulling for Richard.

Before I married my wife, not too many gorgeous women said too much to me. Like I said earlier: life's a learning experience. This 'ole boy ain't no fool. But the *Union 76* girl opened her pretty little mouth and what came out was, "I love those pink stripes!"

As Brisco Darling would say, "That tears it." I'm buying another uniform, no matter how much it costs. This time I'm going with blue.

Now, the only thing I was trying to accomplish is to

finish the race and not tear up the man's racecar. The truth is, he was taking a big chance letting a total rookie drive it. Sometimes in life you take things for granted. Especially when you're young, and don't fully appreciate the extraordinary things people do for you.

When the green flag fell, everything was going real smooth. I even managed to pass a few cars. On lap thirty or so, I saw the leaders coming up behind me. It wasn't until that moment the full impact of the race hit me. For almost twenty years of dreams, starting with my dad taking John and me over to *North Wilkesboro Speedway*, those dreams were being played out at that time when going into turn three I was side by side with "The King".

This time I was smiling ear to ear on the outside, and I didn't care if the whole world saw it! Back then Dover was a five- hundred mile race. Now, it's a one-mile track. So if my calculator is working right, it says that's five hundred laps. Let me double-check that. Yep, that's right, five hundred.

Now back then we didn't have power steering or head restraints. After we had raced what seemed like two hours, the caution flag came out. Only about half the cars had radio communication with their pit crew. We were in the half that didn't.

I couldn't see the scoreboard while we were racing, but under caution I was able to look over and see. I couldn't believe it said lap eighty.

Let me get my calculator back out. That means we had four-hundred-and-twenty laps to go. I didn't want to be the guy with the *NASCAR* record for the earliest relief driver in history. But, the truth was, I was already hurting. I needed a neck like Cale: just a head stuck on shoulders. There ain't no way I am getting out of this car.

Still under caution, the pit crew put up the pit board indicating for me to pit on the next lap. When I came around the fourth turn, I hesitated because I thought I might have been carrying too much speed to turn down pit road. So I went around another lap. It cost us a few positions.

When the green flag came back out after another thirty laps or so, Bobby Allison came around me in turn four. All of a sudden his car was sideways; his left rear tire was going down. At almost top speed, he was in a four-wheel drift and went down pit road. I was amazed!

You can't truly appreciate what some of those guys can do with a racecar until you've been out there with them. As the race started to wind down, so did my neck. It got to the point where I had tried every position to get some relief, but nothing worked. It felt like I had a knife in it. And, my lap times were starting to fall off. That's it. I'm done!

So I patted on my helmet, indicating to the crew that I needed a relief driver. Baxter got in and ran the last hundred laps or so. We managed to finish eighteenth out of forty, with no damage to the car.

After the race, Benny Parsons told me I did a good job. That meant a lot more than you know. I found out later on that six or seven other drivers had relief. It was exceptionally hot for a September day in Dover. During the course of the race I drank two gallons of *Gatorade*.

Baxter said when he put the hose in his mouth to drink a little; he couldn't believe I had drunk the whole cooler dry. The heat wasn't really the problem - it was the G force on my neck. Before I got out of the fire suit, two kids, about ten years old, wanted my autograph. That felt strange.

I wanted to say, "Are you sure?"

But, I just signed them and they said, "Thanks." And so did I.

Then it was time to go home. After a long day of racing and an even longer night of Billy, I crawled into the sleeper. Steve and Billy took turns driving. Billy said I was asleep before we got ten miles down the road.

It's a long way from Dover to Monroe. I didn't remember any of it until Billy woke me up and said, "We 're going through Richmond. We knew you wouldn't want to miss it." I said, "Billy, why would I want to see Richmond?"

About the time I said that I saw our sponsors sign, *Iron Peddlers of Monroe*. We were home.

After unloading the car, I told Baxter, "Thanks."

Then he said something I didn't expect, "You did a good job. Do you want to drive Wilkesboro next week?"

I said, "Sure, I'll come back over tonight and help you get the car ready."

On Friday morning, I left the shop and stopped at *McDonalds* for some breakfast. I remember sitting in McDonalds looking at all the people thinking most of them are probably going to work or to school. But, I am on my way to drive a cup car. Well, like they say, *life ain't fair.*

The 1980 *Holly Farms 400* might be the most memorable race in the history of the speedway, the reason why became obvious minutes after the track opened to practice.

Ronny Thomas spun about the time he went on the track. Then a couple more cars spun. The racetrack surface was breaking up. They stopped the practice session to have a drivers' meeting.

Bobby Allison was the most vocal and said the race needed to be postponed, or canceled all together. The competition director of *NASCAR* agreed to call Bill France Jr. and discuss the situation with him. After talking to France, the competition director said the race would go on as scheduled.

The grove was where the problem was. If you hit it, you spun out. You either had to drive at the very top of the track, or let your left tires practically rub the curb on the bottom.

I managed to qualify twenty-sixth out of thirty cars, but knowing what was coming, I wanted to start out at the back of the field. Bill France Jr. had decided he needed to come up from Daytona to oversee the situation.

When the race started, there was a fifteen-foot gap between the cars on the bottom and the ones on the top. It was a four-hundred-lap race, and one-hundred-and-thirteen were run under caution.

Jody Ridley tried to pass me, lost control of his car, and did a complete three-hundred-and-sixty degree spin, but didn't even lose a position. Every time the caution came out, they would try to clean up as much loose debris on the track as possible. During the last caution, Bill France Jr. was on the track overseeing the cleanup. They were in turns three and four. I noticed a lot of smoke inside the car, but the engine didn't indicate any problem. I looked down where the fire extinguisher was supposed to be; it had broken off its mount and was under the right door roll bars.

So, I came down pit road. The rear end cooler motor had short-circuited. Baxter disconnected it, which took a few minutes. I told Baxter about the fire extinguisher. He said, "If we take it out, they would black flag us."

Back then *NASCAR* didn't have a speed limit on pit road. I was unaware they had moved the cleanup operation down to turns one and two. I carried a lot of speed down pit road, and when I hit the track, I almost ran over Bill France Jr. He went one way, and I went the other. I'm sure it scared him more than it scared me because I was in the car and he wasn't.

I remember thinking: *That's all I need to do is kill the president of NASCAR.*

That would probably be a setback to my racing career. When I caught up to the back of the pack, I thought: *What's this pick-up truck doing out here and where is the pace car?* The track was so bad that the pace car crashed under the caution flag. The pace car spun in turn four, slid down pit road, and hit Bud Strickler's racecar.

You know those times in life where you tell someone not to do something, but they do it anyway? And then what you said would happen, happens? You don't have to say I told you so because what happened said it for 'ya.

I don't know it for a fact, but if you could have seen Bobby Allison's face right then I'm sure there was a smile on it. Bub's pit stall was just a couple down from ours. John told me after the race I had just pulled down pit road when he wrecked. He said Bub's tire changers were almost killed. They were both in the process of changing tires right before the pace car hit. They heard people hollering at them, and they both jumped up on top of the racecar.

Bobby Allison won the race. The driver that by far impressed me the most was Bobby Wawak. If he could have kept from blowing right rear tires, he may have won. He was dirt tracking around the track. There are a lot more factors in winning a race than just driving talent.

After the race, the line to get Wawak's autograph was almost as long as the one for Richard Petty's. I've heard it said: *There's about as many Richard Petty autographs in the South, as there are pickup trucks.* The reason he had so many fans is because even through his success, he never got above his raising. The ten times or so I've talked to him, it was like talking to your neighbor. He generally seemed to enjoy people.

This time I managed a sixteenth place finish without a relief driver.

Baxter asked, "Do you want to drive Martinsville next week?"

Without much hesitation, I said, "Sure."

When we got to Martinsville, we went to where you sign in. The guy who handled that for *NASCAR* was Carl. Baxter asked him how many cars were here. Carl said there were thirty-six cars. They only started thirty-two. Baxter, being the eternal optimist, turned and asked me if I wanted to unload the car or just go back home. I told him I didn't come all the way up here to turn around and go home.

"Let's get the car off the trailer." I said.

Back then the races either had two or three rounds of qualifying. They only took the top twenty at Martinsville in the first round. I was twentieth when the last car, driven by Tim Richmond, bumped me out by three-one hundredths of a second. You could stand on your time if you wanted to, so we did.

A handful of cars were faster than we were in the second round, but we were easily in the field. Jimmy Means missed the race and asked Baxter if he could start our car for points. Baxter asked me, if that would be all right with me.

I told him, "Yeah. But I would like to get in the car at the first caution flag."

When the first caution flag came out, with my helmet on I jumped up on the pit wall to change drivers. Then our car came by with smoke rolling out the windows. We were the caution. The engine had let go. About the only other interesting thing that happened that day was after the race when some drunk started a fight with my younger brother Jody. Jody didn't start it. He just finished it!

The next race was Charlotte. Baxter had already lined up Ferrell Harris to drive. My only plans for the week were to show up on Sunday and change tires. Thursday morning I was in the shop bending roll bars when the phone rang. It was Baxter calling from the speedway. He said Ferrell called him and said something had come up, and he wouldn't be able to drive.

He said, "I need you to get your fire suit and get over here as quick as you can!" Baxter had two cars. The only one I had driven up till now was a Chevy. This one was an Oldsmobile. It was considered a little more aerodynamic; therefore, it should be faster on larger tracks.

Let me point something out. Both his cars were several years old, and I didn't build either one. When practice started I knew I was in trouble on the first lap. The car just didn't have any feel to it. It was like driving a video game without a reset button. I came in and told him I was having a difficult time. I asked him if he thought he might want to drive it. He said he'd rather I did. He just couldn't get around Charlotte.

Back then most of the small independent teams would race on old tires; they just couldn't afford new ones. But for qualifying you always ran new tires or what racers call "sticker tires."

I was kind of in a difficult situation. I could go out there and embarrass myself by going ten to twenty miles per hour off the pace, or go for it and hope for the best. Well, you can't drive a racecar faster than it is capable of going or faster than you are capable of driving it. I chose to go for it.

When I came out of pit road, I gathered speed as I went down the back straight away. As I entered turn three, the car was all over the track. As I entered turn one, the car snapped out from under me. Then I learned something else. I didn't hit the wall, but when the car started down the banking of the turn, I let off the brake.

The car picked up speed like a roller coaster. Because of the radius of the turn and the speed that I had when I came down to the apron of the track, the car came back up the bank and almost hit the outside guardrail in turn two. If it had been during the race, I probably would have gotten clobbered by another car.

The car wasn't damaged. I limped back to the garage area. It was one of those "I told you so" moments. I wasn't smiling, and neither was Baxter. All four of those one-hundred-and-fifty-dollar-a-piece *Goodyear Eagles* were flat. According to my calculator, that comes to $600. For me that's a lot of money. In 1980 that was a whole lot of money.

It's been said that you learn from your mistakes as much as your successes. That's why you can't beat experience. And the only experience I had at Charlotte was five years earlier in a lumber truck. Baxter said he was going to try to find somebody else to drive.

I know this sounds strange, but I had no desire to get back in that car. I knew Bobby Allison, so I discussed the situation with him. One thing about Bobby is that if you don't want it straight, don't ask.

He said, "If you put a rookie in an ill-handling car, the result is going to be bad every time."

Baxter was able to get D.K. Ulrich, a driver with a great deal of experience. We put four more tires on and D.K. went out to shake it down. When he got out of the car, I asked him how it felt to him. He shook his head. "Like a school bus with four flat tires."

This didn't make me feel better; I had a lot experience under those conditions. D.K. was never able to qualify the car, and we missed the race.

That was the end of my racing that year. Over the winter, *NASCAR* made a rule change that made every cup car worth the price of scrap metal. They downsized the cars from one hundred fifteen to one-hundred-ten inch wheelbase. Detroit was producing smaller cars for better mileage.

The only way *NASCAR* could race the newer models was to make the rule change. We were so busy we almost didn't have time for "Fife o'clock." But then again, life's not all about money.

While all of this was going on, my main reason for getting involved in racing was to drive. There was a movie made about this time called *The Right Stuff*. In the movie a guy asked a test pilot what made the program work. The pilot started explaining aerodynamics and physics.

In the middle of his explanation, the guy stopped him and said, "No. What makes all this stuff work is funding. No bucks, no Buck Rogers."

Like I said earlier, there's a lot more to making it as a driver than just driving ability. There's a lot of, (I apologize for having to use a dirty word like this) "politics." You have to use your resources and connections to your advantage.

My dad had retired from *Lowe's* a few years earlier and still knew most of the "Big Wigs." We negotiated with them to sponsor me for the 1981 season, and for me to run for *Rookie of the Year*. Since I hadn't run more than five races in 1980, I was still eligible. They said they would consider it and let me know by a certain date. Now, this was early in, who I consider one of the best presidents of all time, Ronald Reagan's presidency. But, our economy was still trying to recover from one of the worst, Jimmy Carter.

Like I said earlier in this book, I'm going to throw it all out there and let the chips fall where they may. I found out later that *Lowe's* had decided to sponsor me. But right before they told us, their stock dropped a few points, so they delayed their decision a couple more weeks. It fell again, so they decided not to offer the sponsorship at that time.

Like I said, "No bucks, no Buck Rogers."

Baxter had worked out a deal with Slick Johnson to drive his car the first part of the season. Without a ride, I focused on building cars.

Chapter 8

Lord of The Flies

The old building we worked out of didn't have a ceiling, much less insulation. The best we could do to beat the heat was to open the doors and turn on the fans. The war I had with Ralph's rooster was nothing compared to the next plague. Pharaoh didn't have nothing on us.

The shop was in the middle of nowhere, surrounded by cornfields and cow pastures. We looked out across the road. This guy had a manure spreader, and he wasn't afraid to use it. He was putting it on heavy.

I told Jody, "Now we're going to have to smell that crap."

I didn't know it when I said it, but that was the least of our problems. Word spread quickly through the fly world that they were serving lunch at *Dixie Engineering*. The next day we had a least five thousand flies in the shop. I bought fly stripes, but within a few hours, there was nowhere else to land. In desperation, I went and bought several cans of fly spray.

At lunchtime, we would shut all the doors and start spraying at the other end of the shop and back out the door. When we got back to where we began spraying, the first thing we did was get out the brooms and the dustpan. After sweeping thousands of flies, we would start the whole process over every day for about a week.

Now, that's not the kind of place you would expect *Hollywood* and *Ford Motor Company* to contact, but they did. They said in about two weeks they were going to start production on a movie starring Burt Reynolds, Jim Nabors, and Ned Beatty called *Stroker Ace*. They wanted to introduce the new smaller Ford Thunderbird in the movie.

They needed two racecars built in two weeks for the movie. I knew with the financial resources they had, I didn't want to let this deal slip away. But, I had to level with them. With only a three-man operation, there was no way I could meet that deadline. They informed me they had two new prototype cars.

"Could you make them look like racecars?" they asked.

After discussing the logistical problems, we reached a deal. They said they would have the prototypes out at our shop as fast as they could. Speaking of Burt Reynolds and Ned Beatty, when they showed up they probably thought they had found the place where *Deliverance* was filmed. Although, the sign said *Dixie Engineering*, the driver still asked me if he had the right place. With doubt in their minds, and not hearing any banjos, they unloaded the cars.

I was smoking a cigar when I went over to one of the cars and sat down inside. This guy who could have made a living doing the speaking parts of Germans in World War II movies said, "No smoking in the prototypes."

Well, soon we realized that he had a significant role in the development of the cars, and way too much attachment to them. Apparently they hadn't explained to him the full extent of what we were going to do. Now, these two cars were ready to have sales stickers put on them. Instead, we took grinders and a torch to them.

I kind of hated to do it myself, but by the time he left he was pitiful. It would be like buying a new car, and then totaling it on the way home. We gutted the interiors, installed roll cages, and machined an adaptor system so we could put the five-lug, cup wheel on their four-lug bolt pattern. Then we altered the fenders for tire clearance. After a few other refinements, the cars were ready to go. For one of the scenes in the movie, they intentionally crashed and finished off what we had already started.

Burt Reynolds had a friend named Hal Needham who helped produce *Smokey and the Bandit*. They also co-owned the Cup team Harry Gant drove for. A good friend of mine, James Harper, who I still talk to on the phone occasionally, was their head machinist and engine builder. He invented the adjustable pan hard bar bracket. Nowadays, when you see crewmen make chassis adjustment on a pit stop, it's usually that system. He told me they decided to bring an engineer in to see if he could help them with an intake problem they were having an issue with. James said he was a nice guy. While he was studying the intake, James went to the restroom. When he returned, the guy told James he needed to take the intake home with him. James figured he needed to do more intensive research at home, but he would need to check and make sure it would be all right with the crew chief.

The engineer said, "I've got no choice."

Then he tried to raise his hand, but it was stuck inside the intake. Word spread fast and everyone came over to laugh, or to suggest how go get his hand out. James said they considered cutting it off - the intake... not his hand. Before they did, they tried pouring a can of motor oil around his hand. After it soaked in for a minute, it finally came out.

Now James is as strong as a bull, primarily because he has always worked out a lot. His dad died at an early age of a heart attack, and he didn't intend to carry on that family tradition. His first job in racing was with Digard Racing.

Darrell Waltrip was driving for Digard at the time. They were the first team to start a workout program for the pit crew. So naturally they put James in charge of it. Right after they sat the gym up, Darrell came by and said, "It's about time y'all started getting in shape."

James kinda' took it personal. So, he told Darrell he would make a bet with him on who could do the most push ups.

James told Darrell that after he finished, then Darrell could stand on his shoulders while he did his.

Darrell said, "I don't have time right now, but I'll come back later."

Well, he never showed. I guess Darrell didn't earn the nickname *Jaws* for nothing.

Chapter 9

He Throws Like a Girl

That summer somebody came up with the idea that the drivers should start a softball team for charity. For the most part the name fit. It was called *NASCAR All-Stars*. Then they let me play, but since they already had t-shirts made up they didn't want to change the name. They could have taken a Sharpie and put *Mostly* in front of *NASCAR*. I guess they figured that might look kind of tacky, so they just left them like they were.

During *Coca-Cola 600* week, we played the network that was televising the race. I think it was *CBS*. I remember Ken Squier was their pitcher. The charity was for a guy who was having some medical issues, LeRoy Yarborugh. He was no kin to Cale.

At one time he drove for Junior Johnson. Richard Howard, who owned *Howard's Furniture* and was general manager of *Charlotte Motor Speedway* at the time, generously offered to donate two-hundred-and-fifty dollars for every run scored and a five hundred dollar bonus if anybody could hit a home run.

I remember most of our players. Buddy Baker was on first. Who was on second? No, he was on third. Donny Allison was on second. Well, anyway, the rest of them were Neil Bonnett, Darrell Waltrip, Benny Parsons, Tim Richmond, Bobby Allison, Dale Earnhardt, and Joel Stowe (Who?) Well, that's where the *Mostly* came from. For all those people who say racecar drivers are athletes, none of them were at that game.

If you people ever want to figure out where the phrase *He throws like a girl* came from, start at Mallard Creek Ball Field, Friday, Memorial Day weekend, 1981. It will save you a lot of time. Wait, 7pm. All right, play ball!

Now parents like to brag on their kids, no matter how old they are. Now, that I have got kids and the sweetest most beautiful grandkids in the world, (See what I mean) I understand that more. Well, my parents didn't have a lot to brag about when it came to my racing career, but when it came to softball they were as proud as peacocks.

They had a temporary softball fence in front of the baseball fence. The first time I came up to bat there were two men on base, and I hit the ball over the softball fence.

The second time I came up I got a hold of it, and it cleared the baseball fence at three-hundred-and-thirty feet. John told me after the game that there were a couple of guys sitting in front of my parents. When I hit the second home run one of them said, "Who's that guy?"

"I don't know. Maybe it's Rick Wilson," the other one said.

My mom tapped him on the shoulder and straightened him out. By the end of the game, I had two home runs and six RBIs. I ain't telling all this to sound braggadocios, well maybe I am. But, what was ironic about it all was I was on the field with a bunch of millionaires. I probably didn't have more than ten dollars on me and not much more in the bank.

After the game I was feeling kinda' proud. No, actually I had the big head. They had another game after ours. *Howard's Furniture*, which was the world's slow pitch softball champions, played the *Men of Steel*.

There was a guy on Howard's team called *Rick the Rock Crusher*. He hit a ball over the baseball fence... over the light pole... across the parking lot, and halfway up the trees on the other side. While everybody else clapped, I could feel the swelling in my head going down.

After forty years of softball, I finally gave it up a couple years ago. It finally got to the point where the level of frustration was greater than the gratification.

Solomon said, *"There's a time and a baseball season for everything."*

We kid ourselves sometimes. But, when you're in your mid-fifties, you're not going to compete in that kind of sport with people in their twenties and thirties. The older I get, the better I once was.

Chapter 10

No Brakes, No Problem

In Cup racing there is always a few races that seem to draw more enthusiasm than others. One of those is definitely the night race at Bristol. It was getting late in the season, and I hadn't been able to work out a deal with anybody to drive. My plans were as usual; show up on race day and change tires.

Then the call came. It was Baxter. "Do you want to drive my car at Bristol?"

It would be like somebody asking, *do you want a free trip to the Bahamas?*

My first impression of the track was this must be where they train Kamikaze pilots. To turn fast laps at Bristol, you just forget about being smooth. Just mash the gas and hold on!

About the time I started getting the hang of it, the engine let go. Baxter only had one more engine in the truck. He said that's the one he wanted to run at Darlington. He just wanted me to qualify the car, get in the race, and park it after the first lap.

I told him, "If that's what we need to do, that's what we would do."

Not too long after that, Dick May, who was with *STP*, said there was some guys up from Gastonia, North Carolina who were having a hard time getting their car up to speed. They wanted to know if I would be interested in driving it. They were a couple of brothers with the last name Satterfield.

There were only a few minutes left in the last practice before qualifying, so I didn't have time to shake it down. When I came out of pit road, I drove hard into turn three. When I hit the brake, it was the wreck that almost happened. The car jumped to the left. I came down pit road. One of the Satterfield boys walked up to the car with a wad of chewing tobacco.

He leaned in the window and asked, "What's wrong?"

I said, "There's something bad wrong with the brakes on this car."

He said, "I forgot to tell 'ya. The right front rotor is busted in half, so I disconnected it."

I told him, "That might be something I would have wanted to know."

When I got out and looked at it, he had cut the brake line and pinched it off with a pair of vice grips.

I told him I'd not seen anything like that, even when I was running hobby division on half-mile dirt tracks, much less a Cup car. Well, it became a personal challenge to see if I could get the car in the race.

Baxter said, "Cecil Gordon said he would qualify his car and park it when the race starts."

There were thirty-three cars in qualifying trying to make a thirty-car starting field. When we went out to qualify, the car turned about 10,000 RPMs. I thought he must have put the wrong gear in, but I just kept it on the floor.

My brother Jeff said everybody at the track stopped what they were doing to watch. When I came in, we discovered the clutch was slipping. We were thirty-one out of thirty-three. I couldn't believe we out qualified anybody. I told them it was a good effort, and we almost made it. They started loading the car on the trailer.

In the last practice before the race, Gary Balough's throttle hung, and he stuffed his car in the wall. He didn't have a backup car and withdrew from the race. Knowing we were the first car to miss the race, I asked *NASCAR* if we could start. When they said yes, I ran to the pits and stopped the Satterfield boys right before they exited the track.

I said, "Boys, we're in the race. Get the car ready."

They started scrambling.

A couple of hours before the race started, the one who had the chewing tobacco, came up to me and said, "We have a problem."

I said, "You have my full attention. If you don't consider not having brakes a problem, what do you consider a problem?"

He said, "We borrowed a gear from Buddy Arrington to qualify, and he wants it back to race with. The only gear we have left is a Rockingham gear. Do you reckon we could just run it in third gear?"

Let me call another time out. I know a lot of you, especially race fans are thinking... B.S. If this guy took an enema, you could bury him in a matchbox. Folks, Ernest Hemingway couldn't make this up. If I could, I wouldn't write a book; I would have sold investments to Bernie Madoff.

When the race started, we got black flagged around the tenth lap for running slow. Somebody I knew tried to give me a hard time about it. In my defense I said Dale Earnhardt would get run over if his car was in third gear, the clutch was slipping, and he didn't have brakes on the right side of his car.

Well, now that I think about it, maybe not Dale, but almost everybody else. Now after a story like that, I know this is easy for you to believe, but with that effort, I didn't earn *Rookie of the Year*. Well, there's always 1982.

Chapter 11

Daytona USA

Over the winter I worked out a deal to drive *Daytona*. Yes, I said *Daytona*! Now, that's a whole new deal. The simple truth is that back then, that place would put you in the ground if you weren't careful, and it might if you were. Now, if you were to ask me if I was scared, of course not, I was a racecar driver. If you're a racecar driver you NEVER, ever say you're scared. If you're scared you should be doing something else. You use code words like: *concerned or antsy*. If you wanted to push the limit, you might go as far as saying: *I'm tense*.

If I was to admit to anything, I might say, "I have the butterflies."

Did I have the butterflies? If there were any more in my belly, somebody would have yelled, "It's a miracle," because my feet would have been off the ground.

Me and Jody loaded up the car on an open trailer and pulled it with my pickup. Junky Joe and Wayne, a couple of the local boys, decided to go down and watch. If you looked around Joe's place long enough, you would find some pretty neat stuff. But it's mostly where the name came from.

Again, if you *American Pickers* are near Waxhaw North Carolina, stop by and see Joe. If you don't leave with any stuff, you will at least leave with a lot of laughs.

Joe had a paint and body shop. I went over to his shop one time, and he asked me if I wanted some coffee he had made. I did until I saw a heavy layer of orange paint floating on top.

I said, "No thanks; I prefer cream."

He just drank away. Now that I think about it, I haven't seen or heard from him in years. You *American Pickers* might want to call ahead first.

Now Wayne was just out of high school. I don't think he had ever been out of Union County, much less to the beach. Now at Daytona, you could drive on the beach.

When the boys finally got there, Joe said Wayne got out of the truck, ran about one-hundred yards up the beach, turned around and ran about two-hundred yards the other way. Then he came back to the truck and said, "It's a lot bigger than I thought it would be."

Now at *Daytona*, unlike any track I had run up till this time, you're required to get a physical before you race. I don't know why. I guess they figure if you're going to get killed, they want to make sure you are up to it.

When I walked into the infield hospital, it just so happened A.J. Foyt was in front of me. A few seconds later, Richard Petty walked in behind me. They started having a fifteen-minute conversation with me in the middle.

Winston Churchill once said, "No one can make you feel

inferior without first getting your permission."

Well maybe not, but he didn't say anything about feeling uncomfortable. I mean, I would have felt privileged to have been there, but I would have preferred to be on the other side of either one of them. I was already nervous enough without all this. No, that's not it. I already had enough butterflies, without all of this.

The nurse asked the usual bunch of questions. Then one I didn't expect. The last question was "What religion are you?"

For a second I got ready to ask her why she asked that, but I didn't because I knew I wouldn't like the answer.

Now, for me the butterflies were the worst when you were going about sixty miles per hour. You come off the fourth turn, the pace car shots down pit road, and you're looking for the green flag to fall. You think: *The next time I come by here I will be going about one hundred eighty five miles per hour, and surrounded by a bunch of lunatics.* You know they're lunatics, or they wouldn't be out there.

The day of the race Joe and Wayne were in the stands. Joe said the first thing Wayne said when he saw the track was that it was a lot bigger than he thought it would be. Wayne, wherever you are, I hope you heard that on your honeymoon.

I don't remember the first time I saw the beach, but I'll have to admit the first time I saw *Daytona*, I said, "It's bigger than I thought it would be."

We didn't have a sponsor, so Clyde took some duct tape and put *Junky Joe* on the side of the car. Now this was the *Arca 200*. For the next two hours and two hundred miles, it kind of reminded me of that chariot race on *Ben Hur*. Smoke. Flames. Ambulances. You name it; we had it!

If anybody could say they won, it was Joe Ruttman. I finished tenth. I was happy with that, but I was happier just to still be breathing.

After the dust all settled, Junky and Wayne came down across the track. When I saw Joe, I could tell that he was about to bust with pride. He said he figured when I hit the big time I would have forgotten all about him. I told him he was the first guy to sponsor a car at *Daytona* and not know it until after the race started.

Wayne said while the race was going on, Joe finally saw the duct tape and jumped up and pointed at the car and yelled, "That's me. I'm Junky Joe."

Wayne said half the people in the grand stand jumped up, thinking there was a wreck.

Now this was on Sunday during speed week. We didn't have any plans past the *Arca* race because we didn't know if we would still have a racecar, or a driver for that matter.

In those days, the rules for the *Arca Division* and *NASCAR'S Cup* were almost identical. Matter of fact, the car I was driving was one of Ronny Thomas's Cup cars. I decided to stay and run the one-hundred-twenty-five-mile qualifying races for the *Daytona 500*. It was a long shot, but like I said earlier, you will never make a hole in one if you don't swing at the ball.

All my brothers had to go back to work, so I stayed by myself. The races were not going to be run till Thursday. Because it was speed week, there were no hotel rooms available, even if I could afford one. I just bummed rooms from people I knew.

The first night I stayed with a guy named Charlie. Charlie had a friend who was coming down from Charlotte tomorrow, but I could have his bed tonight. Every night, I slept somewhere different, including two nights in the cab of my truck.

When you're practicing, it's common practice to come down pit road and let *Goodyear* check your tire temperatures. This is important information if you know what you're looking for. Since I didn't much of the time, I usually took it to Bobby Allison.

After you get the tire temperature data, your crew would push the car back to the garage area. Since my crew was three-hundred-miles away, they weren't much help.

Once a fellow saw a car I built and said, "You're a genius."

I told him that was with a capital "J."

Nobody has called me that since. But, nobody has ever

accused me of being weak. All the other teams had at least three or four people pushing their cars around. Now it's not easy to push a three-thousand-seven-hundred-pound car by yourself - even if it is on level ground.

Up till this point, my racing career had gone mostly unnoticed, but this seemed to draw a lot of attention, even a few photographs.

After I had pushed the car back to the garage area about the third time, a fellow I had known for years came up to me and asked if I was by myself. His name was Bobby Gene Cooper. He was the oldest son of the legendary Bob Cooper. Now, you probably never heard of Bob, but if you raced *Winston Cup* back in the sixties you would have. Your survival would have depended on it.

He drove in sixty-four Cup races without a win. His record was 0-64. But, when it comes to fist fights, he was 64-0. He had arms like tree trunks and didn't mind using them. He's just one of those people that would rather die than back down to anything.

Now, don't get the wrong impression of Bob. Almost everybody really liked him... but most, ain't everybody. Those few avoided him like the plague. Or a better way to say it is that they avoided him like a compound fracture.

He had a garage in Gastonia, North Carolina. I was at his shop one day, and he looked like he had been run over by a bush hog. I asked him what happened.

He said, "A pack of dogs came in my yard and jumped on my old dog, Joe. If there's going to be an ass kicking at my place, I'm going to get in on it."

So, he dove into the middle of 'em.

I told him, "We've all heard of a pack of dogs attacking a man, but whoever heard of a man attacking a pack of dogs?"

He said, "Well, you have now."

A mad dog is one thing, but a mad Bob Cooper is another. The dogs quickly realized they were in real trouble and started retreating. He said he chased them bastards all over the neighborhood. I knew I could out fight 'em, but I just couldn't out run 'em.

Now like I said earlier, when somebody tells you something, there are only two things to consider: who said it, and what they said. Knowing Bob, I was as sure of this as I was when I was five and my momma told me she loved me.

Now, Bobby Gene wasn't as ornery as Bob, but he made up the difference by being bigger. He was kinda' a younger version of Big Moe. A one-man pit crew, or wrecking crew. Whichever, one was needed at the time.

Other than fistfights, Bobby Gene was also a good engine man. But, whatever he did to the motor, every time I went on the track to practice, our speed was no better than one-hundred-seventy-seven-miles-per-hour. So, I sought out Bobby

Allison's advice again. Like I said, if you don't want it straight, don't ask him.

Instead of telling us to load it up and go home, he asked me how it was handling. "I can hold it wide open all the way around the track," I said.

He said, "If that's the case, put softer springs in the rear of the car. That will get the rear spoiler out of the air more, and you should pick up at least two or three miles per hour."

At about the same time as we got the back of the car jacked up, they closed the garage area. The next morning we changed the springs and started looking over the car to make another run.

Now, a racecar has what's called a dry sump oil system. As soon as the oil goes through the motor, it's pumped out into a large tank behind the driver. When Bobby Gene looked in the top of it, he said it was low on oil.

After we poured about 3 quarts of oil in it, we started the engine to let it warm up. It didn't take but a few minutes to realize we had a problem. Oil started coming out around the valve covers. After a couple more minutes, we figured out what the problem was - stupidity and physics. At least we were smart enough to figure that much out.

When the back of the car had been jacked up all night, some of the oil flowed down into the motor. Well, if stupidity and physics got us into trouble, maybe it would get us out. We came up with a plan. Bobby Gene would get under the car and take the oil plug out of the bottom of the tank, and I would look in the top of the tank and tell him when to put the plug back in. As soon as he took the plug out, hot oil hit his hand.

I heard, "Damn, that's hot," and he dropped the plug into the drain pan.

Another law of physics is four gallons of oil can't fit in an eight-quart container, no matter how much you wish it could.

I kept hollering, "Put it in."

He kept hollering, "I can't get it."

All we could do at that point was let the laws of physics run their course. Oil came up over the pan, and a river of hot motor oil flowed under the three cars beside us. Well, we weren't quite the slowest car in the garage area, but there was no doubt we were the most unpopular.

When I headed off to *Daytona*, I didn't expect to come home feeling like Richard Petty, but I didn't expect to feel like Joseph Hazelwood either. In case you're wondering, he's not a racecar driver; he was the captain of the *Exxon Valdez*.

After a few choice words from our fellow competitors and fifty pounds of oil dry, it was cleared up without an environmental impact study.

Finally, it was Thursday - race day. *Winston Cup* drivers always considered the one-hundred-twenty-five-mile qualifying races at *Daytona* as the most dangerous races of the year. I wasn't too concerned. In the *Arca* race most of those drivers didn't have much more super speedway experience than I did. In this race, I knew if I got in trouble, they weren't likely to run over me. Maybe the reason they were concerned was because of me running over them!

When we were pushing the car through inspection, they were nit-picking us to death. One of the inspectors put a template on the right front fender.

He said, "That's not good enough. If you want to race, it will have to be changed."

The fender was about a quarter inch low in the middle; I figured I would try to pull it up by hand. Like I said, I'm a pretty good size fellow, but the fender didn't budge. By now Bobby Gene was starting to get agitated. He came over and grabbed it with both hands. There was a loud groan followed by a loud pop.

He looked at the inspector, and he just looked at Big Bobby and said, "Okay."

He didn't even put the template back on to see if it fit. I guess the inspector thought that could just as easily been his neck.

I started the race on the last row. I was doing all I could to hold on to the draft at the back of the pack. After just a few laps, right after I came off turn four, the engine got louder and picked up RPMs. I thought it was about to blow, so I pushed in the clutch and shut it off. Now after a while, at those speeds you start to lose some of your sensation of how fast you are really going. I was able to coast two and a half miles around the track. When I got all the way back to turn four, I was on the apron of the track, going about thirty miles per hour.

There's quite a pucker factor when you're going that slow, and packs of cars are only thirty feet away from you going about one-hundred-ninety-miles-per-hour. I didn't look in the mirror because I didn't want to see what might be coming.

My crew of one, Bobby Gene, started looking over the car. He discovered the exhaust pipes had fallen off. So I fired it back up and headed back out. When I came off turn four, I could see the leaders coming up behind me. The lead pack went by me, and Cale Yarborough was in the middle of it. The back end of his car was going back and forth at least six inches.

I could see his hands sawing just as frantically, eight inches in both directions, trying to gain control. I thought, *Look at that!* He didn't gather it back up till he was almost in turn one. As amazed as I was at his ability, I was more amazed at the fact that he never cracked the throttle. Cale might have been short in stature, but measured by heart and guts, he was ten foot tall.

It wasn't like racing today. It was dangerous. I finished

twenty-sixth out of thirty-two. Only the top fifteen cars transferred to the *Daytona 500*.

Another thing that was different then was the radical concept that the fastest cars should race on Sundays. Today, you can show up and qualify faster than another car. He stays and races while you load up and go home. I don't know what it is, but it ain't racing. Well, I think I do know. It's protecting the big teams and their sponsors from missing a race. It's stuff they do like that, and then they wonder why the stands aren't full anymore.

After the race me and Bobby Gene got in my pickup and rode into turn one and found the tail pipes. The safety crews had leaned them up against the inside retaining wall.

They had a race back then on Friday for the cars that missed the *500*. It didn't pay much, but then again we weren't there to make much money. There were only about fifteen cars that participated in it. I thought right before the race I might as well go for it.

When the race started, I managed to pass two cars before we got to the first turn. After we went around the track one time, I was drafting Steve Moore, and Joe Booher was drafting me. I could see through Steve's windshield a car that was sideways. I got on the brakes, and as soon as I did, Joe hit me in the rear and knocked me sideways.

As I came down the track, I remembered not to let off

the brake. The front spoiler of the car hit the apron before the front tires. It made a tremendous grinding noise, and I remember praying, *Lord don't let me start flipping*. The car spun all the away around; I was going backwards at one-hundred-seventy-miles-per-hour.

Ten days before that was as fast as I had gone forward. Now my front bumper was only a few feet from Joe's front bumper. We looked straight into each other's eyes. His eyes were wide open. I am sure he would have said the same thing about mine. We both did several three-hundred-sixty-degree spins.

That night on the local sports, they showed the wreck. The sports anchor said it looked like we were dancing, but we couldn't decide who would lead.

When the race was over, I managed to finish fifth. Tim Richmond won the race. Slick Johnson was second. Within the next few years, Slick and Joe both lost their lives in separate wrecks at that place.

It was time to go home. I still can't remember when we left, whether it was on our own or they ran us off. When I got home I figured all my winnings and all my expenses. My total winnings were $3300.00. My total expenses were $3600.00.

There's an old saying: *The best way to make a small fortune racing is to start with a large one*. But, it's kinda' like the *Master Card* commercials. The memories were priceless.

Well, I wouldn't go that far, but it was certainly worth more than $300.

I watched the *Daytona 500* from the comfort of my brother John's den. Bobby Allison went on to win it.

In 1995, I met Bobby for the first time since 1983. He couldn't remember me. But then again, as a result of his career-ending wreck in 1988 at *Pocono*, he couldn't remember winning his third *Daytona 500* that year. With all the personal tragedies he's been through, Bobby is an example of the toughness that made our country what it is. His brother Donnie had a career-ending wreck in Charlotte. Bobby never fully recovered from his wreck. He lost both of his sons in accidents, and one of his best friends, Neil Bonnett, in a wreck at *Daytona*. He went through very bad financial times, and him and his wife, Judy, separated. But through it all, he never gave up. It's the kind of courage that is very rare today. Fortunately, him and Judy got back together, and I hope them the best. Like all of us, he has his flaws. But, every time I ever asked his advice, he always went out of his way to help.

Chapter 12

Knuckles

That spring, Roger Hamby asked me if I wanted to drive one of his cars at Charlotte to film a *Mountain Dew* commercial. We built cars for Roger and Sterling Marlin and Lake Speed; both drove for him at one time. I could write a whole chapter about Roger, but the best way to describe him is "Slim Pickins." He looks a lot like him and he acts like him.

When I saw the director, I knew he wasn't from around here. And when I heard him speak, I am glad he wasn't. I have to be careful how I say this. We came from two different worlds, and the truth be known, he probably didn't want to be in mine anymore than I wanted to be in his. I just decided I would shut up, mind my own business, and drive.

We were only going about eighty-miles-per-hour, so they sat up a camera on the track in the fourth turn, about eight feet from the wall. I was surprised how many laps we had to turn just to make a thirty second commercial.

I was wondering what happened to the guy who ran me off the track seven years ago. Well, to try to break up the boredom, I got right next to the wall and turned down right before I hit the camera. When we finally came in, I did something I said I wasn't going to do. I asked the director how he liked that shot.

He said, "Oh, that was just savage." At that point, I wondered why didn't I stick to my original game plan.

By the time summer came around, our business had slowed down to where I had a chance to go out West. One of my best friends growing up was a guy named Dart. We got to know each other playing football in junior high.

Dart is one of those names that you really don't need a last name. Nobody ever asked me, "Dart who?"

It's kinda' like the name Elvis. He's the only guy who's got it, probably cause who else would want it? Of course it could be worse. His wife's name is Melanie, but everybody calls her Mule for short. I think I might be in trouble, but that's all right. I've been in it more in my life than I have been out of it.

So, since I am already in trouble...

When me and Dart were in junior high, one of our friends whose name I won't use because he's still trying to recover from what I am about to tell you.

Let it go Knuckles. Let it go. It's been over 40 years now. Let... it... go! How did he get the nickname Knuckles? Well, I'll tell 'ya. When you reach puberty, it's only natural to start taking a real interest in the opposite sex. This can sometimes be awkward to anybody especially when you are fourteen.

Two girls asked Knuckle's and Dart's brother over to eat supper. While trying to make small talk, Knuckles was kinda' nervous. Because of his awkwardness, he started scratching his knuckles. One of the girls asked him what he was doing. He wanted to say, "Scratching my knuckles." But because of his nervousness, he swallowed in the middle of knuckles.

What came out was, "I'm scratching my nuts...Knuckles...Knuckles... Knucklesssssss!" And to think he just about had it all behind him.

Well, anyway, me and Dart decided to venture out to Washington State to see his brother Ralph. We took the back glass out of my pickup and threw a camper shell over the bed. I took the mattress off my bed. One of us drove while the other one slept. Fifty-three hours later we were there. When we arrived it was about 3 AM.

For the next three days the sun never came out. Now, I've always had a pretty good sense of direction, I'm not talking about direction in life like listening to your guidance counselor. I never was much good at that. I'm talking about east and west. Well, I guess subconsciously I had established directions.

On the fourth morning when we went outside, I asked Dart why the sun was coming up in the West. From that time till the time we left, I was as lost as Satan.

While we were out there, the locals got up a softball game. Even though my parents missed the game, I hit a long one. The other team accused ours of bringing in a lumberjack. When I told them I wasn't a lumberjack, they looked at each other and said, "Yeah, I don't believe he is from around here."

Dart's brother Ralph was a physical fitness nut. Although he had a perfectly good pickup, he decided to ride his bicycle from Washington State to Charlotte. It took him about 23 days. I told him that seemed like a dumb thing to do.

He said, "No, it wasn't dumb, it was difficult."

Dumb is kinda' like when you decide to drive a school bus through a river. The only thing I can say to that is, Knuckles, we all have things we would like to forget. "Let it go!"

When we got back from our adventure, I didn't have any more to do than before I left. Only now I didn't have any money to leave again. That's how it always goes. When you have the money to go someplace, you don't have the time. And when you have the time, you don't have the money.

The problem was racing. It was going through a transition, and we were on the wrong side of it. The sport was rapidly growing, and the small independent race teams weren't able to grow with it. The days of pulling a racecar with a pickup and a couple of volunteer crewman in it were all but gone. And those teams were seventy-five percent of our business. Plus, the big teams were starting to build their own cars. There really wasn't enough work to keep all three people busy. So, Bobby started another business doing general metal fabrication, and Jody went to work for some guy at Lake Norman doing motorboat repair.

I started looking for some work outside of racing. I knew a fellow who had a red 1958 Corvette. The steering box was worn out, and he was unable to find another one. So he asked me if I could take one off a Camaro and figure out a way to make it fit. After I finished, I took it for a test spin. A very long spin. I mean it's not everybody whose got a '58 Corvette Convertible. It drew a lot of attention - whether you wanted it or not.

I was sitting at a red light and I heard, "Coe-vett!... Coe-vett!"

I looked around. This 300-pound black woman was running toward me waving her arms.

My immediate thought was, "This is a convertible and she's coming in this car. And how in the hell will I ever get her out?"

There were only two options: ride her around a few hours, or run the light. I wish all decisions in life were that easy. After a quick glance at traffic, I was gone. At *Daytona*, I didn't look in the mirror afraid to see what might be coming. This time I wanted to see what was going. The disappointment on her face wasn't as great as the relief on mine.

Chapter 13

No Bucks. No Buck Rogers

Seven months after racing at *Daytona* I got an unexpected phone call. It was Baxter. He wanted me to drive his car at Wilkesboro. It was just about as easy a decision as running that red light. The car I was going to drive was one I had built him last year. D.K. Ulrich had driven it a few times and told him it was the best handling racecar he had ever driven.

Qualifying was a lot more interesting in those days. There were no provisionals; they actually let the fastest cars race on Sundays. For the big teams it was all about getting good starting positions. For the small teams it was all about making the race. There was more pressure on us qualifying than there was on race day.

Wilkesboro only started thirty cars, and there were about thirty-four there. We managed to qualify twenty-second. When the race started, the first time Richard tried to lap me, I gave him all the racetrack I could. Coming off the fourth turn, he let the left side of his car rub on my right. As he went around me, his rear bumper hooked my front bumper. We both got a little sideways, and as we went down the front straight away, I decided to see if I could keep up with him.

For about six or seven laps, I stuck to his back bumper. Then something I didn't expect happened. I got black-flagged. I knew I wasn't running too slow. Not having radio communications with my pit, I figured they might not like me running with the King.

A few years after Richard retired from driving, he ran for Lieutenant Governor of North Carolina. It was expected to be a close race, but right before the election, Richard got into a bumping incident with some guy on the road. They say it cost him the election. Now, I will admit there are a lot of things I don't understand, and this is one of them. He got into me at Wilkesboro, and I deemed it a real honor to swap paint with the King.

When I got to my pit stall, Baxter leaned in and said the car was smoking. There was a small crack in the oil pan, and there was no way to fix it. So on lap fifty-seven I was done. I didn't know it at the time, but when I got out of that racecar I would never get into another one.

Like I said, "No bucks. No Buck Rogers."

Baxter and all the other small teams would be out of business within the next couple of years. My dad didn't see me run my first race, but he was in the stands at my last. Jeff said when I was running with the King, Dad was saying to the guy beside him, "That's my boy in that car." Maybe I did give him a little to brag on.

Over the years I kinda' changed my perspective on my racing career. Was it successful? That depends on how success is measured. To measure anything you have to have a least two points of reference, where you start and where you finish. Twenty-two years before, I sat in those same grandstands - a six-year-old boy dreaming of racing with the King some day. And I did it.

I wasn't born into racing. All I learned about it I basically had to learn on my own. If circumstances had been different and I had gotten that *Lowe's* sponsorship, would I have had a longer more successful career? Almost certainly. But it wasn't meant to be.

In the movie *Forest Gump*, Forest says, "Life is like a box of chocolates; you never know what you're going to get." The only problem with that is, everything in the box is still chocolate, so how bad could it be? In real life sometimes you bite into a rotten potato. When you do, you got to keep pressing on.

I had some offers to work for some other race teams, but I kind of liked to make it on my own. What really surprised me was when *Lowe's* finally decided to get into Cup racing some ten years later, they didn't call me. For some reason they went with Richard Childress then eventually Rick Hendricks and Jimmy Johnson. I figured they had probably lost my number. I can say I have no regrets towards racing, just fond memories.

It's been thirty years since that race, and I still have a dream now and then that Baxter calls me up and asks, "Do you want to run one more race?"

Now that I'm a grandpa my dreams have shifted from me to my kids and grandkids. Within six months I sold most of my equipment and moved on to something else.

Chapter 14

Black Belt, Black Belt!

Before I got into racing, I had some experience in construction. And since the housing market was starting to recover, I figured that was as good as anything else.

I met my cousin Keith, at my cousin David's funeral. It's a shame it often takes tragedy to bring people together. I hadn't seen him in twenty years. Keith said the only thing he knew about me and my brothers was that we were good boys. Grandmaw constantly reminded him, especially every morning after he came back from a night of partying.

I asked him one time if he had had any trouble at the bars. He said the best he could remember, just once. He didn't remember all the details, but he jumped up and this other guy jumped up and people started yelling, "Black belt... black belt!"

He looked at them and said, "You bunch of nuts; I ain't no black belt!"

I asked him what happened then.

He thought for a couple seconds and said, "That's the last thing I remember."

I said, "You came to the conclusion they weren't talking about you?"

Keith said, "I didn't have a conclusion; I had a

concussion."

Keith sounded just like the kind of man I was looking for. So, we started framing houses. Keith opened us a checking account. When I saw the checks for the first time, they said *C & E Construction*. I said, "Since my name is Joel Stowe and yours is Keith Bowman, what does C & E stand for?

He said, "Close enough."

Every time someone wrote us a check they would ask what C & E stood for. And I would say, "Close enough."

Then they would smile and say, "What does it really stand for?" And, I would say the same thing. Then the smile would go away, and they would just look puzzled. We did good work; we just didn't take ourselves too seriously. I'm glad they always asked the question after we finished, instead of when we started.

After the first year of business, we had all the work we wanted. But to tell you the truth, I missed racing - especially from a driving stand point. I needed something to feel the gap. Then something came along. Me and Keith framed a house for a guy name Gary. Gary had a plane parked beside his house at an airport called *Bradford Field*. It was just a little grass strip in Huntersville North Carolina. I told him I was always interested in learning to fly. Gary said he would be glad to teach me.

I told him, "Don't say it unless you mean it."

Now I'm not going to tell 'ya Gary's last name because

I'm sure the *FAA* would like to discuss a few things with him. If I had to do it all over, I would rather have Evel Knievel teach me to fly than Gary.

For my first lesson I showed up one Saturday. Gary said, "Let's get started."

Before we took off, Gary said somebody tried to tell him it wasn't possible to do a loop in a Cessna 172.

He said, "I don't believe it? Do you?"

I said, "I've got no idea. This is my first lesson. I hope it's not my last."

Gary said, "Let's give it a try."

I said, "What if he's right?"

He hesitated for a second and said, "I tell 'ya what. I'll see if I can borrow a couple of parachutes, then we'll give it a shot."

All Gary could think about was proving the guy wrong. He didn't consider even with parachutes on we might go into a flat spin of which we probably wouldn't be able to get out. And even if we did, at the very least we would destroy a thirty-thousand-dollar airplane.

And, how about this? *Have you or a loved one been injured in an accident, which was no fault of your own?*

I can hear the phone conversation now. "Daggett and Associates."

"Yes. My husband was cutting grass Saturday, minding

his own business, and an airplane with no body in it landed on him. Do you think we have a case?"

It's a scary thought that somebody would need me to use logic and reason before they do something.

The first cross country trip we went on me, Gary, Bobby Penniger, and my brother John were going to a fly-in in Cleo, South Carolina. We were about one-hundred-fifty-pounds overloaded. I didn't know anything about it. I figured if your plane has four seats... that means you can fly four people. When we started down the runway, it didn't take long to realize we were in trouble.

Pilots have a saying: *When you're in trouble you can't use the runway behind you... the sky above you... or the gas that is still in the truck.*

I wish most of that gas was back in the truck. When we finally left the ground, we were over halfway down the runway. The trees at the end of the runway were about a thousand feet away and about fifty feet high. We were no more than ten feet off the ground.

The only thing you can do is pray, and since I wasn't flying the plane, I did. This is no exaggeration. We didn't clear those trees by more than a foot. I've come close to dying many times, but never closer than that day.

For the second trip Gary said he was flying back from Florida one time and saw an island down below, Hilton Head,

South Carolina. Now the only way you could get to it was by boat, unless you're Gary. He called to find out when low tide was.

He said we would just land on the beach. He calculated if we left at 8 AM, we would arrive there at low tide. When it was time to leave, there was only about one hundred yards of visibility because of fog.

Now for most of you that aren't familiar with flying, there are basically two kinds of flying: VFR and IFR. VFR means Visible Flight Reference, and IFR means Instrument Flight Reference. If you're only a VFR pilot, you're not allowed to fly in conditions that limit your sight to less than 3 miles. But that never stopped Gary. He predicted when we got up a few hundred feet we would break through to clear weather. As soon as we took off, I could barely see the wing tips.

I asked him, "How do you keep from running into another plane?"

He looked over at me and said, "Who's stupid enough to fly in this stuff?"

Made sense, so we just kept going. Of course we had no choice. We could never have found the runway. It was exciting landing on the beach. There was no trace that anybody had ever been there. I'm sure it looked the same way it did five-hundred-years ago. There were a lot of palm trees and live oak trees with Spanish moss on them. It was one of the most beautiful places I have ever seen. We filled up a grocery bag with sand dollars and conch shells in about fifteen minutes.

A few weeks later the plane developed an oil leak around some rubber O-rings. Gary asked me if I would help him fix it. Now legally you're not allowed to do any major repair on a plane unless you're a licensed airplane mechanic. But then again, they had their rules, and Gary didn't have any. Besides, it was just O-rings, that's not major repair - even though we had to tear half the engine down to get to them. Gary kept asking me questions about what I was doing.

I kept saying, "I don't know."

He said, "I thought you knew a lot about engines since you used to build racecars."

I told him I wasn't a mechanic. I was a fabricator. If you want roll bars welded into the plane, I was the man. But, I don't know anything about airplane engines.

We had half the motor laying on a sheet of plywood before we started putting it back together. When we finished we didn't have any leftover parts, so we decided to give it a whirl. Gary got in and it started right up. We might have gotten killed when we took off, but at least we saved around a thousand dollars.

One day, after I got my student pilot's license. I decided to take the plane up for a spin. When I tried to start it, the battery was dead. I came up with another plan and once again it came straight out of hell. You can start a plane by hand by spinning the prop. The only thing is you need two people: one to spin the prop, the other at the controls of the plane.

Well, since I couldn't be at two places at one time, I turned the ignition on and sat the throttle at where I thought it needed to be. I figured what can go wrong? The wings are tied down.

When I spun the prop, she sputtered but didn't fire. It was obvious she needed a little more gas, so I reset the throttle. That worked better than expected. The plane lunged forward as I fell back. The stake that the right wing was tied to came out of the ground, and the plane started going round in circles.

When I was kid, I mean a real kid not just acting like one, I had one of those toy planes that was on a string and went around in circles. It was kind of like that, except not as much fun, but certainly more exciting. I was running around in a circle trying to get in the door. Once this was accomplished, it was my turn to look around a couple times to see if anybody saw what happened. When I realized I was in the clear, I got out, untied the other wing, and flew around a while.

Our plane was a Cessna 172, probably the most common plane in the world. The next time I went to Gary's to fly; the Cessna was gone. In its place was a newer Mooney.

When Gary saw me coming, he came outside and told me he had bought a new plane, and he was just going to give us his share of the Cessna. I asked him if he was sure that's what he wanted to do. He said yeah and that he had already taken it over to the hanger and tied it down.

It wasn't but a few months later that the bank foreclosed on his house. They also took his plane and both his vehicles. The same day a friend of his drove him down to the local Chevy dealer. Gary picked out a new truck. When the salesman asked him how he would like to pay for it, he said he would just finance it through the bank.

It was the same bank that had just taken everything he had. To his surprise the paper work went right through. The address he gave was the one the bank just took. I doubt he ever made a payment.

Like I said: *They have their rules, and Gary didn't have any.*

My brother Jody saw him a few years later at a restaurant and asked him if he was doing any flying. Gary said he had just crashed a floatplane in the Bahamas. He had taken some girl to a secluded island. He noticed the waves were starting to get bigger and decided they better leave while they still could. He thought they were in the clear, but the last wave shot them straight up into the air, and they hit tail first.

They managed to hold on to the plane till some commercial fisherman could rescue them. He said that they wouldn't take them back to port till they finished fishing. So they just helped them fish for a couple days. He said it was a lot of fun.

It was just like him; he had already forgotten about the plane and moved on to something else. He was one of the most carefree, or careless, people I've ever known. And that's saying something.

I got my pilot's license in 1986. Now, I know this is not a comforting thought to my fellow pilots. I know how they feel. We have all been at the DMV thinking: *Oh my God. I'm driving on the same road as all these people.*

I was dating a girl named Diane. She was an airline stewardess for *American Airlines*. I was telling her about how crazy Gary was, and she told me a story that topped all of mine.

In the late 1970s, before they had any real airline security, they were flying back from Cancun. They could smell a very unpleasant odor, so Diane and the other stewardesses started trying to locate it. When she opened the door to the closet, she knew it was coming from in there. She unzipped one of those bags you carry over your shoulder. The first thing she saw was gray hair and the back of a woman's head. She said she almost screamed but managed to zip it back up, then told the captain. They were in route to Dallas, Fort Worth Airport. The captain called the controller and told him the situation. When they landed everybody had to disembark in a special location without being able to leave the room.

108

One guy finally came forward and said it was his grandmother. They had gone to Cancun on vacation. She had died of natural causes and when he called the airline to see how much it would cost to have her flown back, he thought it was too high. So he decided to carry her himself. Like I said, you couldn't make this stuff up.

Chapter 15

Coon Heads

The year 1986 was also the year I had one of my accidents. Me and some of the local fellas decided to buy some of those three-wheelers the government eventually outlawed the sales of. They said too many people were getting hurt or killed on them. We did our part to keep the stats high.

After we got bored of just riding around, it didn't take us long to cut down some small trees and build a racetrack. During one of our races, I tried to pass two guys at one time. The left rear wheel hit a stump and shot me across the track. My foot was hanging over the foot peg when Raymond nailed me.

It was one of those times when you knew you weren't going to shake it off and keep going. I thought my foot was broken, so I told them to leave my shoe on so it could hold everything together. I got in the back of Raymond's pickup, and he drove me over to the Minor Emergency Hospital.

When we got to the hospital, the receptionist took my information and told me to wait my turn. If you ever have to go there, you can get out of the waiting room a lot faster if you start dripping blood on the carpet.

The nurse said, "We'll go ahead and take you."

When the doctor took off my shoe, my sock was soaked with blood. So he just took scissors and cut it off. When he did, half my little toe fell on the floor. He looked up at me, and told the nurse to take my blood pressure. When she did, she said, it was normal.

I said, "Why shouldn't it be? It' s not my heart that's hurting, it's my toe."

He just smiled and said he'd have to call an ambulance to take me over to the regular hospital. He couldn't put my toe back on.

When the ambulance got there, the doctor had put my toe in a small jar of ice. He handed it to me because he knew I wouldn't lose it. Raymond said, "Goodbye." He was going back to race.

The doctor at the other hospital looked at my detached toe and said if he sewed it back on I would probably lose most of the feeling in it, and over the long haul it would probably give me less trouble just to leave it off unless I was concerned about it cosmetically. I had to ask him if he was serious. With a face like this, the least of my concerns is half a little toe.

I had also taken a pretty good shot to the gut in the wreck. He was concerned about internal injuries and wanted a urine specimen to check for blood. Well, I tried but when you don't have to go, you just can't go.

He decided to insert a catheter. I learned something else.

When somebody at the hospital says, "You will feel some minor discomfort," grab on to something; it's going to hurt like hell!

When they finally finished with me, I didn't have a way home. I hated to call my parents because I had finally gotten into a wreck that required a trip to the hospital, and I didn't have on clean underwear. But I knew it would take a couple of days to get back on my feet, and mom's cooking would be the best place to recover.

Like I said, that was *one* of my accidents. Back in 1975, I had just gotten out of high school. I think they were almost as happy for me to leave, as I was to go. My dad had just retired from *Lowe's,* and he came out with a pretty good chunk of profit sharing. He made two major investments: a forty-acre farm and a Lincoln Continental.

I was still living at home and tried to go to work one morning, but my truck wouldn't start. I called Big Moe and he said another driver was out and really needed me to come in. The only option I had was to drive dad's Lincoln.

Dad had a van he usually drove, and he was already gone in it. I asked mom if I could drive the Lincoln.

Reluctantly, she gave me the key and said, "You know how much your dad loves that car. You be careful."

About five miles or so from home I was driving on a perfectly straight road. I saw a Ford pickup coming toward me on my side of the road. I went to the right as far as I could without going in the ditch. I had managed to slow down to fifteen or twenty miles per hour. We were going to hit head on, so I tried to go around him on the left. As soon as I turned left, he turned right. When he was about twenty feet away from me, I closed my eyes and locked my arms on the steering wheel.

Back then most people still didn't wear seat belts and being eighteen, and thinking I was bullet proof, I certainly wasn't wearing one. The driver of the Ford was still going full speed. The sound and the impact were incredible. When I opened my eyes, all I could see was a Lincoln Continental hood. The first thing I thought was *I'm still alive. Matter of fact, I don't think I'm hurt.*

I tried to get out the front doors, but neither one would open. I finally managed to kick open the right rear door. We hit so hard the pickup actually went over the top of the car and landed upside down in the ditch. All the windows were knocked out of the pickup, and the guy who was driving it was lying on the roof.

My first thought was *they're both totaled, him and the truck.* I had jumped to conclusions. When I got to him, he started moving, and James Brown was still getting down on the eight-track. He staggered to his feet; it wasn't as much from injuries as from alcohol.

I asked him if he was all right, and he said, "Where's the guy that was driving my truck?"

I looked around and quickly concluded he was lying. I said, "There wasn't anybody riding with you."

"Yeah, somebody stole my truck and I was riding with them."

I told him he would need to come up with something better than that before the cops get here.

Ironically, we crashed right in front of a cemetery. He went over and leaned up against a tombstone. I started throwing used auto parts off the road so at least one lane was open. When I looked back over toward the graveyard, I saw him on the other side, staggering into the woods.

When the State Patrol officer got there, he asked me if these people had been transported. I assume he meant to the hospital. I told him I was driving the car and the other guy was down there in those woods.

He looked at me and shook his head, like: *Why did I have to get this one*? The cop called his dispatcher with the tag number and he said to me, "He lives right down the road. Get in and we will drive down there."

We sat in his driveway about a half hour to see if he would try to sneak in the house. Finally the cop said, "I'll just take you home and try to catch him later."

Turns out by the time they finally arrested him, he had

sobered up and couldn't be charged with drunk driving. They charged him with leaving the scene of an accident, which was a lesser charge and he avoided losing his license. When we rolled up the driveway, I could see mom looking out the window.

While I was taking dad's golf clubs out of the trunk of the patrol car, she came out and said, "Where is your dad's car?"

I told her what happened and she said, "I told you to be careful."

I said, "You told the wrong guy; you should have told the drunk."

When Dad got home, he walked in the house and said. "Where's my Lincoln?"

Well, I had to go through the whole spill again. Now looking back it seems like all the concern was over the Lincoln.

He said, "Where's it now?"

I said, "The wrecker driver said he was taking it to the Lincoln Mercury place over on Independence Boulevard."

Dad said, "Let's go."

When we got there, I was driving the van and pulled in around the back of the body shop. It just so happened there was a car the same year and color as his. It had some front-end damage consisting of a busted-out grill, headlight and a bent bumper.

Dad said, "Oh my God! Well, I guess it could be worse."

I said, "It is. There's yours over there."

He looked at the other end of the parking lot and was speechless. There was a large gold accordion that was once his prize procession.

Then he finally said, "Son, you could have gotten killed."

The truth is that I am glad I was driving it instead of him or mom. They probably wouldn't have survived it. I had bent the steering wheel about 3 or 4 inches, with my arms absorbing the impact.

While we were scoping it over, the guy that was head of the body shop came out. We started talking to him, and I told him I was driving it. He said the same thing Dad did. He had never seen a car that torn up without the driver being killed or seriously injured. When it was all said and done, Dad came out ahead. The insurance company gave him a newer model with less miles.

Like I said earlier, that was one of his investments upon retiring. The other was a farm. To this day I still don't know why he bought it, and if he was still around he wouldn't either. He knew as much about farming as he did astrophysics. Let me take that back, I don't know what he knew about astrophysics, probably nothing. But I know he didn't know anything about farming.

To get started, he bought about 10 cows. My younger

brother Jeff made an interesting observation; the only thing that was holding up most of the fences was briars and honeysuckles. The only problem with that cows like honeysuckles.

So one night after we were all asleep, there was a knock at the door. I answered it and this guy said, "I think your cows are out."

I didn't see any reason to wake the rest of them up. I figured I could handle it myself. I got in Dad's van and headed over to the other side of the farm. About the time I got the fence up, a neighbor down the road stopped to see what was going on.

His name was Howard Gordon, but because he was a plumber most people called him *Flush Gordon*. He liked to coon hunt and was on his way back to his house. As it turns out, trying to heard them cows back through the gate wasn't as easy as I thought it would be.

I told Flush I was going to the barn to get a feed bucket. If the cows thought I was going to feed them, they would probably follow me. Flush said he had a bucket in the back of the truck, so he handed it to me. I noticed by the weight that there was something in it. Because it was dark, I couldn't tell what it was.

Well, it turned out it worked like a champ. When I got back to the van, Flush had already left, so I just put the bucket down beside me in the van. The next morning when I got to work, Big Moe told me I needed to call home.

Mom answered the phone and said, "Do you know anything about a bucket of coon heads in your dad's van?"

I kinda' laughed and said, "Yeah, I put them there last night when the cows got out. But I didn't know there where coon heads in it."

She said, "Your dad's all tore up; he was afraid somebody was trying to intimidate him."

This time I laughed out loud and said, "Why would anybody try to intimidate him?"

She said, "He had just seen *The God Father*, and in the movie the mafia had cut off a horse's head and put it in some guy's bed to send him a message."

After I hung up, me and Big Moe had a big laugh. Dad was a good man but he had some kind of medical condition. I think it was called anxiety attack disorder. I never could figure out where it came from.

Chapter 16

Dad and Mom

Despite his nervous condition, Dad was an exceptional athlete. He played center field for the *University of North Carolina* in 1951, the same year my older brother John was born. Dad was born in 1922. His dad died of pneumonia when he was only 13. He was the oldest of 7 brothers and sisters in the middle of the Great Depression. *I feel like breaking into a chorus of Patches, but I will try to control myself.*

Jobs were scarce, but he managed to get a job at Newport News, building Liberty ships. He was only about eighteen or nineteen. He sent most of the money home to Grandma. Because he had a job that was crucial to the war effect, he wasn't drafted into the Army until late in the war.

Dad's second oldest brother was Archie, and being so close in age, they were very close growing up. Matter of fact, because I'm second oldest, I'm named after him. His middle name was Leon, and so is mine. Dart is always giving me a hard time about it. But at least Dart, it is my middle name and not my first!

Right before Dad was to be deployed to the Pacific Theatre of the war, he was sent to San Francisco to await deployment. The day before he left, he didn't have anything to do so he decided to just walk around town. He turned the corner, and there was Archie.

Archie was in the Navy and they hadn't seen each other in almost 2 years, and they had no idea where each other were. They had the opportunity to spend the rest of the day together.

A couple of months later, my dad got a telegram informing him Archie had been shot down by a Japanese Zero and was killed in action. Now some people might say, *what were the odds of them seeing each other like that?* I think they were 100%. Odds didn't have anything to do with it. You might disagree with that, but you have the right to be wrong.

After Dad survived the war, he was able to go to college on the GI Bill. After college he went to work at the *Charlotte Observer* newspaper. One day in 1959, he was at work and the man that started *Lowe's* came in to run an ad in the paper. The guy's name was Carl Buchan. They struck up a conversation. Dad said it was one of those times in life where you meet somebody for the first time, but you feel like you've known them for years.

At the end of their conversation, Carl asked Dad to go to work for him. Dad put in his notice that day, and when he got home that night he told Mom they were moving to North Wilkesboro. And he would be making over a one-hundred-dollars a week! They started dancing in the kitchen. It was the money they were dancing about, not moving to Wilkes County.

With his new job he had to do a lot of traveling. Once, while they were out of town, one of the guys came into the hotel dining room for breakfast.

He said, "Did you see that game on TV last night? The quarterback threw the ball sixty-five yards for a touchdown. I don't know anybody who can throw a football that far." Dad said, "I can throw one that far."

Well, this led to a rather strong disagreement. Finally, it was time to put up or shut up. After breakfast they went to *K Mart* and bought a football. They went back to the *Lowe's* parking lot and measured off sixty-five yards.

I don't know if there was any money involved, but if there had been, Dad would have taken it. They estimated it went about seventy yards. Like I said, he was a good athlete.

A few years after Dad retired, I noticed when I would go over to his house that he would ask me the same question two or three times within a few minutes. Within a few months, he was diagnosed with dementia, which later turned into Alzheimer's.

Now let me say that Alzheimer's is a terrible disease. It's as hard on those who have to care for the person who has it as it is for the person who's got it. My attitude has always been: *That's life; good things happen and bad things happen.* It is what it is and with something like that, you can only try to make the best of it. The whole family just pulled together and tried to help Mom through it.

After he had been diagnosed with Alzheimer's, me and my brothers took him to play golf. For those of you who are not golfers, congratulations.

As far as I'm concerned, it's kinda' like those smoking commercials. If you smoke, QUIT! If you don't, DON"T START!

They say it's called golf because when it was invented all the other four-letter words were already taken. Well, anyway, we were playing Captain's Choice. If you're not familiar with it, congratulation! That means you don't play golf.

You divide into teams. Everybody on a team hits their ball, and then they decide which one is best. Then everybody else picks up their ball and hits their next shot beside the best ball. You repeat this process every shot until it's in the hole. If you're confused, think how Dad felt.

Dad and John were the best golfers, so they took on me, Jody, and Jeff. After they hit their drive, their ball was in the middle of the fairway about one-hundred-fifty-yards from the hole. John told Dad to hit that ball, the ball landed in the middle of the green. After he hit it, John dropped his ball where Dad's was so he could hit his. When Dad saw it, he lined up to hit it.

John said, "What are you doing?"

Dad said, "I'm going to hit this ball."

And John said, "That's my ball."

Dad said, "Where's mine?"

John said, "Up there on the green."

Dad looks up there and sees it, and says, "I'm not going to walk all the way up there. I'm going to hit this one!"

He did, and it rolled up on the green a few feet from his first one. Even with Alzheimer's, he was still twice the golfer I ever was.

A year or so later, the condition had worsened as it always does. By this time Dad had lost most of his money in bad investments and was living in a mobile home. Him and John were in the front yard sitting in the swing, when suddenly Dad said, "I just want to go home."

They say with Alzheimer's you tend to lose your short-term memory first and start confusing the present with your childhood. That's why they say to try to leave them in surroundings they're familiar with. But since we believe our Mom was raised by a band of Gypsies, that wasn't happening.

John told him, "Dad, you are home."

He said, "Huh?"

Dad then looked at one end of that mobile home and slowly scanned to the other end and said, "This is my home?"

John said, "Yes, this is it."

Dad said, "Well, shit!" Then, slowly he got up and walked into the house.

Not too many months after that, he went on to meet the

Lord. When he said he just wanted to go home, well Dad, now you are. I look forward to seeing him again, but the next time I see him, he won't have that crap, ever again!

At his funeral, my younger sister Jane got up and told a story about him. When we were living on the farm, we had a couple of horses. Jane was only about fourteen at the time and went to the barn to feed them. She came back running to the house all excited and said one of them had had a colt. We knew so little about livestock; we didn't even know any of them were pregnant. Unfortunately, it only lived a few days. One morning Jane found him dead. The only people at home were her, mom, Jody, and Jeff.

They tried to dig a grave, but when they attempted to cover the colt up, its feet were uncovered. They were just too young to dig a big enough hole. That night Jane came into Dad's bedroom crying. She said she kept thinking about those hoofs out of the ground. Dad told her that he had heard when the Indians buried somebody they wouldn't cover up their feet so they could walk into heaven.

Jane said it wasn't until years later that she realized he lied to her. She said he could have done what most dads would have and said, "It will be all right; just go back to bed." But he was wise enough and caring enough to reach a fourteen-year-old girl who was very upset.

Not long after Dad died at the Hospice house, Jane said

she was sitting at the foot of his bed saying goodbye. Before she left the room, she reached down and pulled the sheets off his feet. I saw full-grown men with tears coming down their face. I'll admit I kinda' got misty- eyed myself.

Now, back when my dad was with *Lowe's*, he had a friend named Max Freeman. He was head of *Lowe's* air fleet. He was quite an amazing fellow. He learned to fly planes when he was just fifteen. His instructor was friends with Amelia Earhart. He had his pilot's license for seventy-five years and over forty-thousand-hours logged. According to my calculator, if you flew four hours a day, it would take you about twenty-eight-years to log that much airtime.

He flew a B-29 Mitchell in WWII. After the war they talked him into joining the Air Guard. They told him; when the war was over and with an officer's commission, he would have it made. Within a few years, the Korean War broke out, and he was called up for service. They put him at the controls of a B-29 Super Fortress.

Once while out on a mission, he was shot down by a North Korean Mig. He said he was able to bail out in the middle of a blizzard. When he landed he didn't know exactly where he was in relationship to enemy lines. He snuck around as quietly as he could and heard some people talking. As he slowly approached, he said he could tell it was English with a lot of cussing. He knew at that point it must be Marines.

He shouted out, "Don't shoot! I'm American!"

He walked over to them, and they said, "Where did you come from?"

He said, "I was just shot down."

You know there's something special about that generation. Somebody once asked former Prime Minister Tony Blair why he was so fond of America.

He quoted John 15:13, which says, *No greater love, hath no man then this, that a man lay down his life for his friends.*

He said, "Jesus Christ died for our sins. And the American GI died for our freedom."

Max lost his wife Ann to cancer. A few years after Dad died, him and Mom started going out together. One day, Max asked her to marry him. She asked me what I thought about it since she was seventy-eight and he was in his mid- eighties.

I told her their age didn't have anything to do with it, as long as they loved each other. I said, "You know you probably won't have too many years together, but that's not important. Just enjoy one day at a time" They married in 2005. Just a few months later they were at the beach, and my mom's back started hurting so bad they had to come home. When she was examined at the doctor's office, they had to tell her she had an advanced stage of cancer.

In the movie *Gladiator*, right before Maximus went into the arena to fight, someone said his odds of survival weren't very good. He said, "Death smiles at us all; all we can do is smile back."

I've never seen anybody handle it with more courage and peace then she did. Her hope wasn't in treatment; it was in John 11:25: *He that believeth in me, though they were dead, yet shall they live.*

The cancer wasn't defeated in her body; it was two-thousand-years ago on the cross. She went to be with Him a couple months later. I hope when death smiles at me, I'll have at least half the courage to smile back the way she did.

Chapter 17

Another Bob

Well, it's time to introduce you to another Bob. This one is Bob Gladden. He's not the craziest, although he's very close. He's certainly the most colorful. It wasn't until now that I realize how many crazy "Bobs" or "Bobby's" I've known. You might want to take this into consideration if you're expecting a child. I'm not trying to tell you what to name your son. I'm just suggesting what you might not want to.

Now Bob Gladden was first cousin to Bob Cooper. In case you forgot, he's the Bob who attacked the pack of dogs. Of course, it's hard to forget a thing like that.

Bob used to help Mad Dog Bob back in the sixties when they were racing. I thought racing was wild when I was in it, but some of the stuff they did made what happened when we were racing look pretty calm.

He said they had a race in Columbia, South Carolina, so all the crews stayed at the same hotel. When they got there, the hotel marquee said *Welcome, all NASCAR drivers, mechanics and car owners*.

When Curtis Turner got there, he drove his rental truck into the swimming pool. Neil Castles rebuilt an engine in his room. Then they knocked down a wall between two rooms to make room for the band. After the race, when they got back to the hotel, all their stuff was sitting on the sidewalk in front of the hotel, with what he figured was half the police department in the parking lot. The marquee now said *Absolutely NO NASCAR drivers, mechanics or car owners*!

Bob said racing didn't pay much back then and what they did win was mostly spent on beer and women. And they wasted the rest.

Well, this is the background Bob grew up in. When Bob was still a teenager, he was working under a racecar that fell off the concrete blocks that was holding it up. He was by himself and was pinned under it for quite a while before his mother found him. As a result of the accident, he lost one of his legs. It was going to take a lot more than that to slow him down.

Bob owned a bar in the 1970s. I never cared much for the bar scene, so out of curiosity, I asked him the same question as I did my cousin Keith, "Did you ever get into a fight?"

He said, "One time I got into it with a guy that wasn't all that big. I figured I could take him. When he started pounding on me, it felt like jack hammers hitting me in the head. When the beating was finished, I crawled over to the door in time to see him get into a pulp wood truck."

Bob said if he ever gets ready to get into another fight, he would make sure to ask the guy if he happened to be in the pulp wood business.

Bob is a true capitalist; he also owns a trailer park. Now for all you *Wall Street* occupiers and haters of our capitalistic system, go protest Bob. He'll have something for 'ya. Well, anyway there was an elderly lady in the trailer park who was having plumbing problems. I'm talking about her trailer, not needing to drink more prune juice.

Bob crawled up under her trailer to fix it. She was standing on the porch watching while Bob was working. Bob said there was a cat around his feet. Actually, it was foot, since he only had one. But he wasn't paying much attention to it.

While he was talking to the lady, she said, "I wish somebody would kill that old cat."

Bob said, "Are you sure? I can make the necessary arrangements."

She replied, "Well, I wish somebody would."

So Bob just took his pipe wrench and popped it in the head.

Bob said she screamed, "What are you doing? You just killed my Persian!"

Bob said, "You said to kill it."

"Not my Persian. That cat." She pointed over his shoulder at an old mangy cat that he didn't even know was there.

Bob said he didn't know there were different kinds of cats, and he also learned that Persians are kinda' pricey.

He said, "That damn cat cost me nearly two-hundred-dollars."

Another time, Bob said he had a guy in the trailer park that was always complaining about how bad his life was. When the guy came down to Bob's one time to pay the rent, he told Bob he tried to kill himself the night before but the gun misfired. Bob said he was tired of hearing it, and he knew he only wanted attention.

Bob called his bluff. Bob reached into his back pocket and pulled out his 38 snub nose revolver and said, "Here, try this one; it works every time!"

The guy stepped back and said, "You're crazy."

Bob said, "How the hell am I crazy? I ain't the one talking about killing myself."

Bob said he never heard another complaint from him.

I guess if you're going to run a five-star trailer park, you've got to be good at psychology, plumbing, and animal control.

About twenty years ago, Bob's other leg started giving him some problems. In spite of everybody telling him to go to the doctor, he just ignored it till the pain was so bad that he had to go. Now for Bob to yield to pain, it would have to be incredible. He's one of the toughest people I've ever known.

When the doctor saw it he said, "That leg has to come off today or you will die."

After the operation, I called him at the hospital. We've always been point blank with each other.

I said, "I hate you had to have your other leg chopped off."

I could tell by his voice, he was in some real pain, but he would never admit it.

He just said, "I figure the next time I buy a bed, I'll save some money by being able to get a shorter one."

Like I've said, I've questioned his wisdom but never his spirit.

Bob's got a vacation place at Oak Island, North Carolina. He asked me if I would come down and help him put a new roof on it. So, me and Billy flew my plane to the island. I would always fly low over it and reave the engine. By the time I got the plane tied down, Bob would be there to pick us up.

Bob was not going to let a small thing like not having legs stop him from helping. At first, he had his prosthetic legs on, but he quickly discarded them. I'm sure it was quite a sight for folks riding by to see a man with no legs, scooting around on his butt, putting on a roof with his legs lying beside him. With the shoes and socks still on them.

Bob said, "I need another bundle of shingles." Well, I couldn't just tell him to go get them. So while I was on the ground, Bob yelled down to me and said, "Bring up that suntan lotion; my legs are burning up here."

134

Bob asked me to run down to the corner store and get him something one time, and he handed me the keys to his pickup. The first left turn the seat slid halfway to the right side door.

When I got back, I told him, "I know you've never put on a seatbelt, but don't you think you should at least attach the seat to the truck?"

He said, "It's easier for me to get in and out of it without legs."

I'll be point blank again, after being around people like Bob most of my life, I've determined most people are candy asses.

Chapter 18

My Bride

The first time I ever saw my wife, Tracy, I had just sat down at a restaurant table.

She came out of the kitchen carrying some plates of food. My first thought was: *That's a cutie!*

Now, at first she didn't seem very interested, but what she didn't know about me is that I'm very hard headed and not easily discouraged. After several trips to this establishment, I managed to woo her with my ways. During our conversations, she found out I was a carpenter, a Sunday school teacher, and I owned an airplane.

Now, for her, and most people, these three don't seem to fit together. Let's face it; we all have a tendency to stereotype people sometimes. She couldn't figure out how a carpenter could afford an airplane. Well, I've always told people who think if you own a plane you must have a lot of money that I don't have much money because I own a plane. Those things will dollar you to death.

Now, I'll have to admit. Most of the people in the construction industry have a reputation for being kinda' rowdy. So, for me to be a carpenter and a Sunday school teacher was a problem for her.

That one was easy. I just said, "Jesus was a carpenter."

Now Tracy is nine years younger than me. And it just so happened I taught her age group. So, I encouraged her to come see for herself. I told her how to get to the church. To my surprise, on Sunday morning she came through the door. At this point I knew she must be interested, so I asked her out.

On our first date, I took her out to eat spare ribs. I was a little nervous but I remembered not to start scratching my "knuckles." We started talking about flying, and she said she had only flown once when she was very young but couldn't remember much about it. I told her if it weren't getting dark I would take her up after dinner.

She said, "Can't you fly a plane in the dark?"

The truth was I had never flown at night and didn't have any night training. So being true to form, I said, "Sure, let's go."

We took off and flew around North Charlotte for a while, but when we decided to fly back to the airport, all I could see was a sea of lights. I had no idea where the airport was, so I called Charlotte approach control and requested direction to *Bradford Field*.

He gave them to me and his last communication to me was, "It's three miles at eleven- o-clock."

Well, I saw eight green lights. So, I assumed that was it. So I headed for 'em, and we landed. That was our first date and my first night flight.

As we got more serious about each other, I figured I needed to put her to the test. The truth is things didn't work out with Diane, the airline stewardess, and me because she was too high maintenance. I decided to fly Tracy to the beach for a weekend fishing trip with Bob at his place. I figured that if she got back home and still wanted anything to do with me, I had found the woman for me. On the way down, there was a small cloud in our way. At least that's the way Tracy saw it.

She said, "Don't you see that cloud up there?"

"Yeah, what about it?"

"You're not going to hit it, are you?"

"No, we're going to go right through it."

Right before we got to it, I could see her brace herself. It's always fun to fly people who have never flown much. Over the weekend we did more laughing than we did fishing. That's usually the case when you're around Bob.

After our fishing trip, I knew I had caught a partner for life, and I would never throw her back. Well, as it turned out, four months later we tied the knot. That was twenty-four- years, three kids, five grandkids and about fifty dogs ago.

Chapter 19

Sand in My Shoes

After one short year of marriage, you know how it sometimes goes. Things don't always go the way you think they will, and we moved to the beach. I know some of you thought I was going to say we separated. I just told you in the last chapter; I had found a partner for life, not to mention, you know now that I think about it, that's a dumb thing to say. How can you: *Not to mention something*, and then turn around and mention it? You're either a liar or an idiot. I say enough dumb stuff without adding this to my vocabulary. If my research department were around right now, (Katy and her computer), I would look up phrases and see what boob came up with that one. Of course, we're just as dumb as the boob for using it, so I ain't going to use it anymore. You can replace all three words with just one and here it is - *Plus*.

Plus, I said I wasn't going to ever throw her back. Plus, do you think I'm going to have three kids, and five grandkids with a woman I don't like? Well, I do take that one back. People do that all the time.

So there were two basic reasons we moved to the beach. First, we simply like the beach. Me and Tracy still go down there about five or six times a year. The second reason was that my brother John told me and Jeff he had all the carpentry work we wanted and he needed some dependable help.

John had always been in construction, usually as a contractor. He had taken a job on Bald Head Island as a superintendent. Now Bald Head Island sits at the mouth of the Cape Fear River beside Oak Island, North Carolina. They say pirates gave it that name because there used to be a sand dune that looked like the back of a bald man's head. And they needed it as a landmark to navigate around, Frying Pan Shoals.

John said the first week he was there he hired a paint sub-contractor named Larry to paint a house. Larry sent two of his men to get started. Later on that day, John stopped by to see how it was going. He said it was one of the crappiest paint jobs he had ever seen.

He said, "Guys, this ain't going to get it. I'm going to have to let you go."

He hired a new contractor named Wayne. A couple of days later, he came into the same house to check on the new crew, and the same two guys were painting.

John said, "What are you doing?"

They said, "Larry fired us, so we called Wayne and asked him if he had any work we could do. He said he had just got a job on Bald Head Island if we wanted it."

John said. "Just keep on going. I can't fight this."

The first day me and Jeff rode on the contractor boat

over to the island.

I told Jeff, "This is about the roughest looking bunch I've ever seen."

It should have been called a pirate ship. They must have been direct descendants.

Jeff said, "If I had a phone, I'd call *America's most Wanted* and tell 'em we've bagged the whole bunch."

Me and Jeff were working on a house, and this woman who lived beside it walked in and said, "I can't believe they're building this spindly little house beside mine. Me and my husband spent a ton of money on our house, and now we've got to live beside this."

I thought: *Ain't you an arrogant snob?* So, I played along.

I said, "I know it. There goes the neighborhood. The same thing happened to me and my wife. We bought an Oakwood mobile home, and the next thing we knew they rolled in a Fleetwood right beside us."

She didn't know what to say, so she just left. The truth is, I made it up. I wouldn't know the difference between an Oakwood and a Fleetwood if they were rolling down the road, but this part's true. I ain't too good to live in either one of them.

One thing I'll say about the people I've mentioned so far in this book. Some of them, maybe even most, might be considered a little rough by most. But none of them are arrogant, disingenuous people. They are who they appear to be. If you like them, that's good. If you don't, they don't care. I don't know about you, but I don't consider myself nothing but a sinner saved by grace. Not by my performance, but by His, and it was perfect. I just asked and received it.

On another house we were doing interior trim, and I heard something down in the basement. It was a ka-plump, ka-plump sound. I went downstairs to investigate. This guy had two empty dry wall buckets tied to his feet. He was reaching into another bucket with a piece of corner bead, scooping up putty and throwing it against the wall. Then he would try to spread out the ten percent that stuck. I thought it might be the dumbest case of vandalism I'd ever seen. At least I would have been halfway right.

Not knowing if he could talk, I asked, "What are you doing?"

He said, "I was working down the road and the superintendent came by and asked if I knew how to drywall. I told him I could, but I was kinda' slow."

I thought: *That's obvious.* Well, just like the woman, I didn't know what to say, so I just went upstairs.

John got a phone call one morning from his plumber.

He said, "John, I'm having a problem, and I'll be a little late getting there."

John asked, "What's the problem?"

He said, "My boat sank. And me and Flounder are sitting on a buoy in the Cape Fear River, waiting on the coast guard. If the buoy hadn't been here, we would have drowned."

Now, I don't wish this on the man and know he's one of God's creatures, but the whole world would have been better off, especially from an aggravation and financial point of view, if God had just let Flounder drown. I guess it's just hard to drown a flounder. If I were as big a screw up as he was, I wouldn't use my real name either. He made Virgil on the old *Andy Griffith Show* look like Bob Villa.

Flounder was installing a drain on a large whirlpool tub. The only screws he had with him were about three inches long.

Jeff said, "Flounder, those screws are too long."

He just said, "It will be all right." He screwed them in and once again screwed it up.

The screws went two inches inside the tub. Because Flounder was too sorry to walk fifty feet back to the truck to get more screws, about eight-thousand-dollars of tub and ceramic tile had to be replaced.

Well, after about a year of this, John had enough and headed back to Charlotte. Not too many months after that, Jeff followed him.

After Jeff left, I needed some help. I ran across a guy named Murphy. I can't remember his last name, and I believe about two hours after work every day, neither could he.

I asked him where he was staying, and he said, "Down on the inter coastal waterway." I said, "That's kinda' of expensive. How can you afford it?"

He said, "It don't cost anything."

He went to Wilmington and bought a surplus life raft at the Army Navy Store. He slept on top of it, and if it started raining, he just turned it over and slept under it. Sometimes I will give people like him a chance because not too many people will, and it usually ends the same.

Well, he was a *no show* one day, but came rolling up the next. I asked him where he had been. He said, he passed out on his raft, and when he came to, he didn't know where he was. He reckoned he had his raft too close to the water and when the tide came in, it washed him down the river about two miles. Plus, he washed up on the other side. He said he finally got a guy in a motorboat to tow him back. Well, I knew he wasn't lying. Who could make that up?

Murphy had a Chevy Cavalier that looked like he took leftover parts from four different cars and put it together. He had a drinking buddy who he hung around with most of the time. One Saturday before the drinking started, they drove up to Wilmington to a petting zoo. They had an elephant there that was advertised as the oldest known elephant in the world. I remember seeing on the news a few years ago that it finally died. They had a little stand there, where you could buy food to feed the animals. Murphy said his buddy started teasing that elephant by holding an apple out and pulling it away right before its trunk got it.

After this process repeated itself a few times, Murphy said, "Man, don't do that."

The next time that elephant reached out, and he pulled the apple back, the elephant blew snot all over him.

He said, "An elephant's trunk holds a lot of snot."

He said it hit him right in the face. It was in his hair and dripping onto his shoulders. Murphy said that's the hardest he had ever laughed. It must have been because he could hardly tell me without laughing.

Murphy worked pretty good when he was there. But he proved to be too unreliable, and we parted ways. You wonder sometimes where people like that go from there.

Chapter 20
Billy

While we were at the beach, I invited Billy to come down and spend the weekend. After a couple hours past the time he should have been there, the phone rang.

I answered it, and I heard, "I'm in jail."

"What are you doing in jail?"

"I got caught speeding through Whiteville, then they got me on a DWI."

I told him I was proud of him. That was further than he got last year. A little sarcasm seemed right at the time.

After the trial, he lost his license for a year and had no transportation, so I told him if he wanted to move, he could work for me. That way I could do all the driving. Billy said he had never done any house framing before, but he would give it a shot.

After his first day he said he had never been so sore and tired in his life. On the ride home we passed by a veterinarian hospital.

Billy said, "Pull in here."

I asked, "What for?"

"I want to see how much they would charge to put me to sleep."

I think he was kidding, but I'm not sure. Since Billy didn't have a license, he wasn't able to cash checks, so I drove him over to the DMV to get a temporary ID. Now, Billy is one of those people that everybody tends to like; he's one of those who will strike up a conversation with anybody. So while we were waiting, and waiting, and waiting, I overheard him talking to an elderly lady.

She asked him if he was getting his license renewed.

"No, ma'am, I got a DWI when I was speeding through Whiteville. I'm here to get an ID."

She looked at him with eyes of sympathy and said, "Did you learn your lesson?"

Without hesitation, he said, "Yes ma'am. If you're going to drink, don't speed."

She looked at him like he was speaking a foreign language.

Billy said, "That's all behind me now. The Lord has forgiven me of that. We all do dumb things when we're young."

I told him I agreed.

"But weren't you 49 at the time?"

"Yeah, but I guess some people grow up faster than others."

I agreed with him again and said; "I guess we're both guilty of that."

Before me and Billy met, he said a couple years after he got married him and his wife decided to buy a house. Billy was self-employed at the time, so him and his wife went to see his accountant at tax time. Billy said he was a little black man that reminded him of Gary Coleman. Billy explained to him that if he was going to be able to get a bank loan, he would need to show he made at least forty thousand dollars last year.

"So how much will I owe in taxes?"

Gary started hitting the buttons on his calculator and said, "About six-thousand-three-hundred."

Billy said, "Well, just forget about the house."

"What if I made thirty-thousand-dollars? How much will I owe?

Gary hit the buttons and said, "About four-thousand-two-hundred-dollars."

Billy said, "We're going at this from the wrong direction. I've got one-thousand-eight-hundred-dollars for taxes. How much did I make?"

Gary hit the buttons and said, "Nineteen-thousand."

Billy looked at his wife and said, "No wonder we don't have a pot to piss in. I don't make nothing."

Then he told Gary to send them off.

Another time on the way back from a fishing trip at Bob's, just about the time we leveled off at sixty-five-hundred-feet, Billy said, "I got to pee."

I asked him why he didn't go before we took off.

"I really didn't have to go then, but I do now."

"Well, try to find something to go in." He found a Styrofoam cup under the back seat.

After a couple minutes of trying, he said, "I can't go in this position."

So he turned around with his knees in the seat and his butt in the air. We started laughing.

I told him I didn't know whether he was coming or going. When I heard the cup, he was definitely going.

After he finished, the cup was almost full.

I said, "You're going to have to hold that for a long time."

He said, "Why can't we throw it out the window?"

"Billy, we're going one-hundred-fifteen miles per hour. What do you think is going to happen when you try to do that?"

After changing hands back and forth about an hour, he said his hands were getting tired.

"Think positive thoughts."

"Like what?"

"How good your bladder feels."

There isn't anything like a beautiful day of flying while the guy beside you is holding a cup of pee. It could have been a lot worse. At least it was a smooth flight.

I was talking to Billy on the phone a while back about

kids these days. I imagine Adam and Eve did the same thing, and it's been going on ever since.

I commented to him, "You don't see kids out playing much anymore. I think they spend most of their time inside on a computer, or playing video games."

Billy said, "It's no wonder we have an obesity problem with so many kids. When I was a kid, I lived out in the country, and the ice-cream truck never came out that far. But when the mosquito truck would come down the road, all the kids would come running and chase it down the road. We enjoyed running through the smoke. When we couldn't keep up anymore, we would stand on the side of the road and cough, catch our breath, and head back to the house."

Maybe sometimes, virtual reality is better than reality.

Chapter 21

The Banjo Man

In 1997, me and all my brothers decided to join forces and start our own company. My oldest brother, John, had fallen in Dad's footsteps and attained a business degree at U.N.C. Jody had extensive experience in construction and had trained him self to be a first rate plumber. Jeff had a physics degree and I always wondered why he helped me do carpentry work. I asked him one time, and he said, "I guess I'm a damn fool." As usual we agreed. And then there was me. I had a pretty good feel for construction and metal fabrication. Together we made a better team than we did on our own, having backgrounds in construction and racing. Plus, with a huge growth in the sport, we decided to join the two together and work for race teams building engine-testing facilities. Well, there's not much racing in Long Beach, North Carolina. So after two and a half years of sand in our shoes, and ten thousand mosquito bites, it was time to leave.

After being gone for over thirty-six years, we settled down in good 'ole Wilkes County. Most of the people around here are good 'ole God fearing country folks who are always willing to help a neighbor. That's most, but we have more than our share of rednecks, lunatics, and outright morons.

For example, a few years back, some woman's boyfriend shot her husband, or it might have been the other way around, I forget. But, anyway, after the shooting, he ran off into a large track of woods. Well, some of the locals decided they were going to take the law into their own hands and go in after him.

They formed a posse. Now the only thing worse than a posse of morons is a drunken posse of morons. They mounted up and headed in. Within seconds a shot rang out. Sounded like they got 'em.

Then one of the posse came running out of the woods and yelled, "Call an ambulance! Lester got shot!"

Well, the only problem was, Lester was one of the posse.

Did he get ambushed? No! He fell off his horse and shot himself! Unfortunately, it was only a flesh wound. After the ambulance left, they decided to turn it all over to the sheriff's department.

After we had been up here a few years, our oldest daughter, Katy, asked for a banjo for Christmas. Well, like many musical instruments, after the curiosity wore off, it just sat there silent and collected dust.

Right before the next Christmas, Tracy decided it was time to sell the banjo and use some of the proceeds to buy this year's Christmas. She put an ad in the local paper but didn't get a call till Christmas Eve.

This guy said, "Are you the people with the banjo?"

Tracy said, "Yes."

He said, "Well, I think I might want to buy it."

Tracy started telling him where we lived. He stopped her and said, " I don't have a driver's license. Would you deliver?"

I told Tracy I didn't want her going over there by herself, so we would just take it together. When we got to his place, what he called a driveway looked more like a drainage ditch. We went up into the woods to where there was an old, dilapidated trailer that was leaning to port. I told Tracy to stay in the truck, and then I got out and started to walk up on the deck to the front door.

I heard from inside the trailer, "That deck won't hold 'ya. Go around back."

About the time I got halfway around his trailer, he met me in the middle. This guy looked about forty, and although the temperature was about the same, he didn't have a shirt on, or shoes, just an old pair of blue jeans.

He said, "Are you the people with the banjo?"

I pulled it out of the case. His eyes lit up like a kid who gets his first bicycle.

He said, "'Ole man," reached in his pocket and pulled out two one-hundred-dollar bills.

He was a nice guy and we talked till his feet got cold, and he went inside. A couple of weeks later the phone rings. As usual, Tracy answers it because ninety percent of the time it's for her.

"Hello."

"Are you the people that sold me the banjo?"

Tracy automatically figured he wanted his money back, and said, "Yes."

He said, "I want to pick you out something."

Tracy listened while he played over the phone.

When he finished, he said, "I know that wasn't too good, but I'm going to keep practicing, and I'll call you back."

He called us about every two weeks to a month for the next four months. When he would call, Tracy would hold the phone up between us, so we could both listen. This is the truth, you could tell a significant improvement every time he called.

I asked him, how much he practiced.

He said, "About five or six hours a day."

If I had to do it all over again, I would have just given the banjo to him. Here was a man who didn't have much more than a banjo and, by what I could tell, was totally content with life. After we hadn't heard from him for a while, Tracy said, "I wonder whatever happened to the Banjo Man?"

I said, "I guess long distant calls from Nashville are kinda' expensive."

Chapter 22

Chicken Crap

Now, there's something I forgot to mention in the first sentence of this book. Wilkes County is also known for chickens. Now, I'm talking about the kind with feathers. Like I said earlier, we got more than our share of rednecks, lunatics and morons, but I ain't seen a coward yet.

I got to know the local bank president from church. I told him I was looking for about ten acres. He called me one day and said there was a good deal on a chicken farm that had thirteen acres.

Me and Tracy took a look at it and even though we knew about as much about farming as Dad did, we bought it. We decided to go all in. My daughter Casey was into horses, so it wasn't long before I had as many as Ben Cartwright. We also got a goat, a sheep, a duck, and a rooster we named Rooster Cogburn, after the movie with John Wayne. We named the duck after the Clint Eastwood movie *Unforgiven*. He was the *Duck of Death*.

The Duck of Death and Rooster Cogburn struck up a real friendship and hung around together all the time. Every day they would walk up to the horse trough, and the Duck of Death would go for a swim while Rooster Cogburn watched. After the swim, they would mosey back to the barn. They were almost as good as Sy.

We named the sheep Wooly Booger and the goat Uncle Nat. Uncle Nat came from the *Andy Griffith Show* when Otis got locked up with a goat that he mistook for his Uncle Nat.

One day Tracy came into the house rubbing her breast and said, "Uncle Nat bit me on the titty!"

I said, "I can't hold that against him. But if you tell somebody, make sure they know he's a real goat and not an old goat." After all, this is Wilkes County. We also bought a pig at a Myrtle Beach pet store. When we got her, she was just a cute little piglet. She squealed all the way home. I wanted to name her Ned Beatty, after his performance in *Deliverance*. But she was a female, so we thought Myrtle was best.

Now at the same time, me and my brothers had our company; me and my bride took on the responsibility of raising about thirty two thousand chickens.

The way it works is you're a sub-contractor for a poultry company. They bring you the baby chicks and supply all the feed. For the next six to seven weeks, your responsibility is to raise them in preparation for the kitchen table.

Now our income is based on a complicated formula. It's basically how much your birds weigh when they're delivered to the processing plant. And how much feed you used. If you had asked me how much feed I would need for my first flock, I would have said, "I don't know. I'd rather have too much than not enough. Give me ten-thousand-pounds." We ended up using over four-hundred-thousand-pounds!

You also are competing against the other growers in your region, and some of your pay is determined on where you rank compared to them. We did the best we could with that first flock, but when we got our check, and our ranking report, we were twenty out of twenty-one.

Tracy was disappointed, but I said, "Baby, there's some poor idiot out there that knows less about chickens than we do." Like I said, we've got a few morons in the neighborhood.

Where we go to church there was guy named Eddie. He was also in the chicken business. He's gone on to be with the Lord, but before he left, he came out of church and said to me, "I guess you've heard the animal rights people are starting to protest the chicken industry."

My response was, "*I thought God smote the Amorites*, now how are they protesting anything?"

He said, "Not Amorites, animal rights!"

It's no wonder the rest of the country makes fun of our Southern accent when we can't even understand each other.

I was at work one day, and Tracy called me and said, "You need to come home. One of the water lines in the chicken house busted, and we have a mess."

When I arrived, there were about one thousand chickens

stuck in about four inches of wet chicken crap. Like I said earlier, most of the people up here are good, 'ole country folk who are willing to help a neighbor.

Our neighbor Ted came over and lent us a hand. We had to stick our hand underneath the chickens, grab them by the feet, and pull them straight up. When we did this, they would frantically start flapping their wings and chicken crap would go all over us.

I was proud of Tracy; she hung right in there for the next four hours till we were finished. Now, by what I just described, you would draw the wrong picture of her. Ted's brother Leon, that's his first name by the way, paid Tracy about as high of a compliment as a woman can get around here.

He said, "She is as cute as a speckled pup."

I don't know how an old fart like me got her, but I'm just glad I did.

We were at a restaurant one time. Tracy was ordering the food, while I was sitting at the table. A guy asked Tracy, "What is your daddy's name?"

She said, "Richard, how do you know him?"

He looked over at me and said, "I know him from somewhere."

Tracy laughed and said, "That's my husband."

He was with the other 'ole geezers who gathered there every morning for breakfast. I could see them looking and laughing from across the restaurant as he told the story.

When we got up to leave, he said, "I'm sorry."

I said, "Don't be. That's a compliment. That means I did real good; she's the one with the problem."

Ted and his wife Joanne asked me and Tracy to go to a place that served BBQ, and after the meal there would be square dancing. Well, the BBQ part sounded good, but I had doubts about the square dancing.

Now, I'm about 6'4, two-hundred-thirty-pounds, and Tracy weights less than half that. I hadn't danced since high school, but they talked me into giving it a whirl. When we started, I was being too rough with my bride. Tracy eventually ran off the dance floor and Joanne took off after her. Me and Ted just looked at each other and said, "What's wrong with them?"

So we just started square dancing with each other. Some of the rednecks started cheering and throwing money. It was the hardest two-dollars and seventy-five cents I ever earned. And that was before we split it.

After three years of trying to work with my brothers and run a chicken farm at the same time, we decided to get out of the chicken business. With our old chicken houses and broken down equipment, we always ranked near the bottom. No matter how hard you try, you can't make chicken salad out of chicken crap. Now they just hold junk and provide a home for Myrtle and Uncle Nat.

We found Rooster Cogbun dead one morning. We don't know what got him, but after examining the murder scene, it was obvious he put up a hell of a fight. That afternoon, the Duck of Death just flew off, never to be seen again.

I feel confidant my son Garrett won't follow in his Dad and granddad's footsteps and buy a farm. When he was about ten, he showed me some pictures he had drawn, and it was obvious God had given him a special talent.

Not long after that a woman not far from our place tragically lost her two-year-old daughter in an accident. Garrett drew a sympathy card for her with a picture of an angel flying towards heaven, carrying a child. You could see the girl's feet on one side of the angel and long blonde hair on the other. The mother constantly looked at it until the funeral and right before they closed the casket, she put it inside. It's amazing how much a small amount of our time can touch someone else's life in such a meaningful way.

Folks, it's time to wrap it up. It's taken me fifty-six years of life to write this book. It's probably the only book I will ever write. I doubt the good Lord will give me another fifty-six years so I can have enough stories to write another one.

Like I said earlier, Ernest Hemmingway wouldn't make this stuff up, and I sure couldn't. Thank you for reading it. I hope you enjoyed reading it half as much as I did writing it.

I want to thank all the people who made it possible. And I would like to dedicate it to my bride, Tracy. She's had to put up with a lot. And now that you've read it, I'm sure you would agree.

The End.

Wait!

One more thing... "Let it go Knuckles," "Let it go!"...

Text copyright © 2012 Joel Stowe

First Edition December 2012

Printed in the U.S.A.

ISBN-13: 978-1481219617

ISBN-10: 1481219618

21514206R00096

Made in the USA
Lexington, KY
15 March 2013